CLASSIC CHRISTIANITY

in

Words and Pictures

BOB GEORGE

HARVEST HOUSE PUBLISHERS
Eugene, Oregon 97402

Cover by Koechel Peterson & Associates, Minneapolis, Minnesota

Illustrations by Aaron Schmidt

CLASSIC CHRISTIANITY IN WORDS AND PICTURES
Formerly *Classic Christianity Illustrated*

Copyright © 1993 by Harvest House Publishers
Eugene, Oregon 97402

Library of Congress Cataloging-in-Publication Data
George, Bob, 1933–
      Classic Christianity in words and pictures/ Bob George
            p. cm.
      ISBN 0-7369-0495-6
      1. Christian life—1960–   2. George, Bob, 1933–   .   3. Christian life—Caricatures and cartoons.   I. George, Bob, 1933–   Classic Christianity.   II. Title.
      BV4501.2.G42   1992
      248.4—dc20   92-30777
                                                                                                              CIP

Printed in the United States of America

02   03   04   05   06   07   08   09   / BP-CF /   10   9   8   7   6   5   4   3   2   1

Contents

Part 5
Identity

Part 6
Law and Grace

Part 7
Dependency

Part 8
Truth

Part 9
Freedom

Introduction

Jesus is and was the greatest teacher who ever lived. Those who heard Him said that He taught with authority. And anyone with a teachable heart, from the youngest person to the oldest, could understand the depths of His message.

Throughout the Gospels Jesus used physical illustrations to teach us spiritual truth. For example, He pointed to a vine and branch to show us our need to live in dependency upon Christ. He described the different types of soil to teach us about man's heart, how it responds to the gospel, and which type will produce fruit. For those who heard Jesus in person and for us today who read the Word of God, physical pictures help plant spiritual truth deep in our hearts.

The world that we live in is full of examples that can point us to a deeper understanding of God's love and grace. That is how I have learned most of what I know today about my personal relationship with Jesus Christ. Throughout my 24 years as a child of God, God has embedded the truths of His Word in my heart through showing me an illustration either in nature or through one of life's circumstances. These illustrations have been so helpful in my own spiritual growth that I decided to use them to teach other people as well.

Several years ago I was introduced to a young man by the name of Aaron Schmidt. Aaron was a schoolteacher at that time and asked if he could volunteer during the summer months to help in our publications department. We quickly discovered Aaron's artistic abilities. During those summer months he started drawing on paper the verbal illustrations that I had been using in my teaching. We quickly converted those drawings into overheads, and I began taking them to teaching assignments all across the country. After each seminar, numbers of people approached me and asked how they could get a copy of the illustrations. We received so many requests that we decided to publish them in book form.

This collection has 31 of my favorite illustrations. These can be very effective tools both to help you understand the depths of God's love and grace and to help you explain the gospel to others. Each illustration stands by itself and explains one aspect of the gospel. We have placed them in an order that progressively explains the fullness of the gospel. We begin with the pictures that point out the deity of Christ and end with those that explain the freedom that we have in Him.

This book can be used in many ways. First, as the subtitle explains, it is a visual aid that explains the truth of the grace of God. As such, it can help to deepen your understanding of the truth of God's grace in your own heart. Second, the book can be used as a teaching tool to help you communicate the gospel to other people. Finally, *Classic Christianity in Words and Pictures* is an excellent tool for teaching the simplicity of the gospel to your children. The number-one question that we receive from people is, "Is there anything available to help teach the grace of God to our children?" I think this book is a great place to start.

It is my hope that God will use this book to deepen the understanding of His gospel message in the hearts of Christians all across the country. He has used these illustrations in my own life, and I pray that He will use them in yours as well.

Jesus Christ

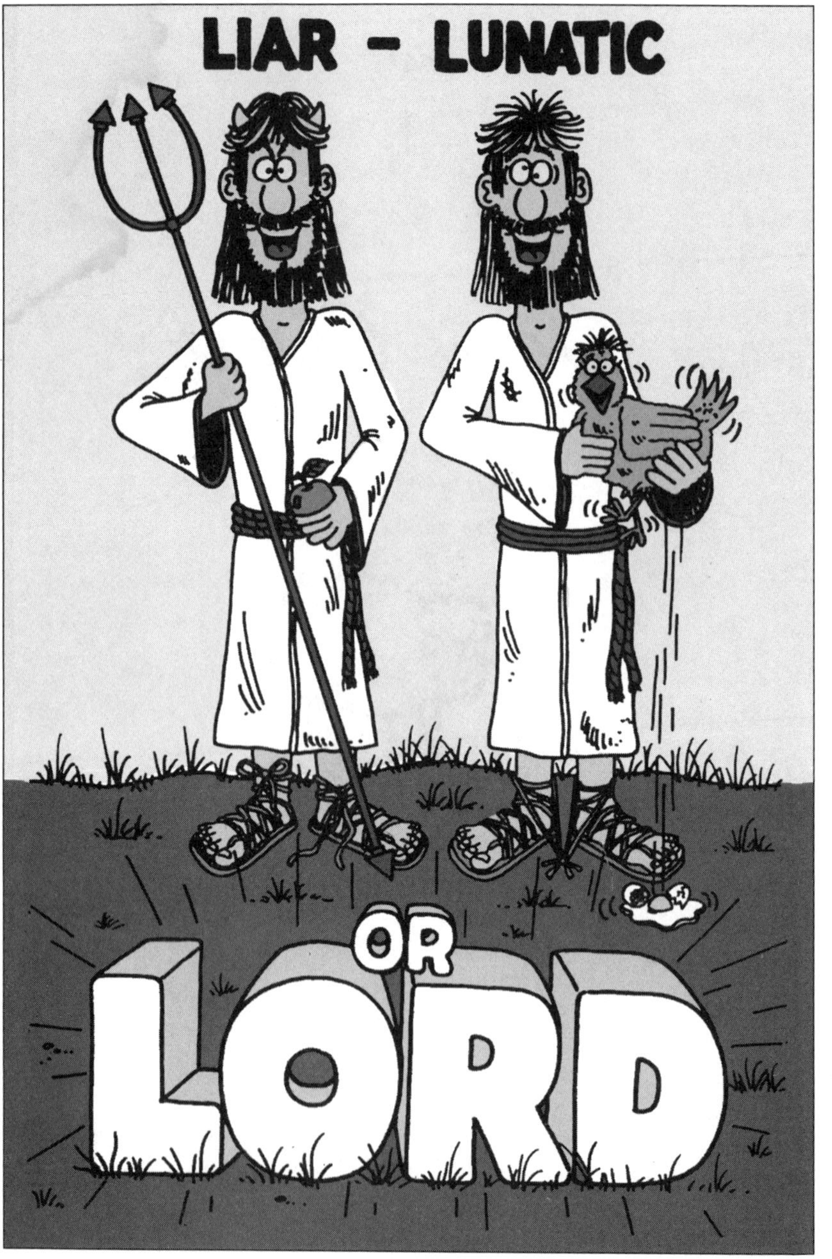
LIAR - LUNATIC
OR
LORD

1

Liar, Lunatic, or Lord?

When Jesus came to the region of Caesarea Philippi, He asked His disciples, "Who do people say the Son of Man is?" They replied, "Some say John the Baptist; others say Elijah; and still others, Jeremiah or one of the prophets." "But what about you?" He asked. "Who do you say I am?"

Matthew 16:13-15

If you were to visit anywhere in the world today, talk to men of any religion, and ask, "Who in your opinion is the most outstanding personality of all time?" you would most likely get the answer "Jesus of Nazareth." No matter how devout they may be or how committed to their particular religion, if they know any of the facts, they will have to acknowledge that there has never been a man like Jesus of Nazareth. He is the unique personality of all time.

He is the One who has changed the whole course of history—so much so that someone once described history as "His story." Remove Jesus of Nazareth from history, and it would be a completely different story.

But who is this Jesus of Nazareth? Is He a great moral teacher as some have said? Is He a great religious leader, like Buddha or Mohammed? Or is He a prophet like the prophets of the Old Testament? These are the answers many people have given about Christ's identity. Are these accurate conclusions, however, based on what Christ claimed concerning His identity?

Upon examining Christ's claims, C.S. Lewis observed in his book *Mere Christianity:*

> A man who was merely a man and said the sort of things Jesus said would not be a great moral teacher. He would either be a lunatic—on a level with the man who says he is a poached egg—or else he would be the Devil of Hell. You must make your choice. Either this man was, and is, the Son of God: or else a madman or something worse. You can shut him up for a fool; or you can spit at Him and kill Him as a demon; or you can fall at His feet and call him Lord and God. But let us not come up with any patronizing nonsense about His being a great moral teacher. He has not left that open to us. He did not intend to.

As C.S. Lewis wrote, Christ's claims were so outrageous that they leave us with only three options. Jesus was either a liar, or He was a lunatic, or He was the Son of the living God.

Jesus Christ claimed to be God. Throughout the Gospels He said things like, "I and the Father are one" (John 10:30), and "Don't you know Me, Philip, even after I have been among you such a long time? *Anyone who has seen Me has seen the Father*" (John 14:9). He made many other statements concerning His identity. That He was coming through loud and clear is evidenced by the response of those who heard Him make these claims.

To His statement "I tell you the truth...before Abraham was born, *I AM!*" (John 8:58), the Jews picked up stones to stone Jesus. They knew exactly what Jesus was claiming concerning Himself. In Exodus 3, God met with Moses and appointed him as the one who would lead Israel out of Egypt. Moses wanted to know what to say to the Israelites if they asked God's name. God said to Moses, "I Am Who I Am. This is what you are to say to the Israelites: I AM has sent me to you" (Exodus 3:14). Jesus Christ was claiming to be the God of Abraham, Isaac, and Jacob.

These same Pharisees on a later occasion picked up stones again to stone Jesus. When Jesus asked for which miracle were they stoning Him, they replied, "We are not stoning you for any of these...*but for blasphemy, because you, a mere man, claim to be God*" (John 10:33). And when Jesus told the Pharisees, "My Father is always at His work to this very day, and I, too, am working," the Bible records that the Jews tried all the harder to kill Jesus. The reason was that Jesus was not only breaking the Sabbath, "but He was even calling God His own Father, making Himself equal with God" (John 5:17,18).

The Pharisees knew that Jesus was claiming to be God. Their response makes it clear that they did not agree with Jesus. Their response to Christ also makes it clear that they did not conclude that Jesus was a great man, or a good moral teacher, or even a prophet. He was someone they felt they must kill, not because they felt He was a threat to society, but because He was a threat to them. "If we let Him go on like this, everyone will believe in Him, and then the Romans will come and take away both our place and our nation" (John 11:48).

Another group of people responded in a totally different manner to Jesus than did the Pharisees. The apostles and the writers of the New Testament, like the Pharisees, heard Jesus coming through loud and clear. Matthew, Luke, Mark, John, Paul, Peter, and the writer of Hebrews all wrote that Jesus was and is God. Unlike the Pharisees, however, these New Testament writers did not try to kill Jesus. They proclaimed that He was God, and they took His message to the world. As a result, they were ridiculed, mocked, and most of them were killed. To them it was impossible to conclude that Jesus was merely a great man, a moral teacher, or a prophet. Jesus is the Lord God, and these men gave their lives to Him.

Those people who heard what Jesus claimed concerning Himself did not conclude that He was a great moral teacher or a prophet. Jesus' claims forced them to conclude that He was either a liar, a lunatic, or God in the flesh. These are the only options available. Many people throughout history have made all sorts of statements concerning the identity of Jesus: a religious leader, miracle worker, a great teacher, or a prophet. However, once a person is confronted with Christ's claims, he is forced to decide among the same three options as the Pharisees and the apostles.

Jesus asked His disciples, "But what about you? Who do you say that I am?" His question remains for us to answer today. Who do you say that Jesus is? After examining the facts, are you willing to accept Jesus Christ for who He is—God? If so, are you willing to give your life to Him? In Christ you will find everything you are looking for. He says to each of us:

> Come to Me, all you who are weary and burdened, and I will give you rest. Take My yoke upon you and learn from Me, for I am gentle and humble in heart, and you will find rest for your souls. For My yoke is easy and My burden is light (Matthew 11:28-30).

2

The Hindu and the Anthill

*In the beginning was the Word, and the Word was with God,
and the Word was God....The Word became flesh and
lived for a while among us. We have seen His glory,
the glory of the one and only Son, who came from the Father,
full of grace and truth.*

John 1:1,14

Until I was 36 years of age, I believed that Jesus Christ was the Son of God. I didn't know what that meant. However, I believed it so strongly that when one of my fraternity brothers in college denied that Jesus was the Son of God, I punched him out. Like me, all of us have some opinion concerning Jesus of Nazareth, whether right or wrong.

The Bible says that Jesus is God. But how could God become a man—and why? This is very difficult for us to understand. To many people, the very fact that Jesus Christ came to earth as "one of us" proves that He could not be God. Therefore, His death on the cross has little significance. To them, He was just a good man who died a horrible death. However, the apostle Paul wrote,

> Although He existed in the form of God, [He] did
> not regard equality with God a thing to be
> grasped, but emptied Himself, taking the form of

a bond-servant, *and* being made in the likeness of men. And being found in appearance as a man, He humbled Himself by becoming obedient to the point of death, even death on a cross (Philippians 2:6-8 NASB).

A number of years ago, several college students shared the gospel with one of their classmates who happened to be Hindu. The Hindu student knew that there was a God, yet he could not grasp the Christian concept that God actually visited this planet in the person of Jesus Christ and then died to take away our sins.

One day while walking through a field and wrestling in his mind with this concept of God, he observed an anthill that was in the path of a farmer plowing his field. The particular sect that he belonged to believed that all life was sacred: a cow, a cobra, even an ant. Gripped with a concern similar to what you or I would feel for hundreds of people trapped inside a burning building, the Hindu wanted to warn the ants of the impending danger. But how? He could shout to them, but they would not hear. He could write to them, but they would be unable to read.

How then could he communicate with the ants? Then it struck him. Out of sheer love, he wished that he could become an ant. If this had been possible, he could have warned them before it was too late. Then he realized this was what his Christian classmates were trying to tell him about Jesus.

At last he understood how God had called to mankind, but we wouldn't listen. He wrote to us, but we refused to read. Out of sheer love, Jesus Christ—Himself God—stepped out of heaven and took on a body of human flesh. He became like us and lived a perfect life. He led us away from death and destruction by becoming a sin offering in our place. He demonstrated His love for us on a cross. It is through His death that we escape the penalty for our sins.

Why did God become man? He did so to save us from our sins and then to give us His very life.

Have you settled in your own mind the truth of Christ's perfect humanity and complete deity? Are you willing to trust in what He did for you as your only source of salvation? As the apostle Paul said in Romans 5:8, "But God demonstrates His own love for us in this: While we were still sinners, Christ died for us."

3

The Sheepdog
and the Shepherd

*Now while He was in Jerusalem at the Passover Feast,
many people saw the miraculous signs He was doing and
believed in His name. But Jesus would not entrust Himself to
them, for He knew all men. He did not need man's testimony
about man, for He knew what was in a man.*

John 2:23-25

Therapy seems to be the answer for everything these days. Therapists, psychologists, or psychiatrists—the so-called experts of the day—appear on TV and radio talk shows almost daily, giving Americans the "answers" to all their problems. And those persons in therapy talk about it as if it were a status symbol. Americans have gone counseling crazy. Christians are not excluded from the counseling craze either. What appears on Christian TV and radio is not much different than network programming. We simply dress up the worldly solutions in a Christian suit.

In light of this counseling craze, what role should Christian counselors play in the lives of believers?

My wife, Amy, received a call one night from a friend of hers. This friend needed advice and counsel for a particular circumstance in her life. Amy talked with her several hours, explaining that Christ was the answer to her problems. At the end of the conversation, her friend wondered about going for more counseling at People to People and asked whether or not Amy thought she needed to. Amy said yes because "They are like a *bunch of sheepdogs herding the sheep back to the shepherd.*"

This is the best illustration I have ever heard describing the role of Christian counselors. We do not have the answers to life's problems. But as Christians we know Someone who does. And our role is to point people to Him. There are several reasons why.

First, Jesus Christ created you and me: "For by Him all things were created: things in heaven and on earth, visible and invisible, whether thrones or powers or rulers or authorities; all things were created by Him and for Him" (Colossians 1:16). Because Jesus Christ created us, He knows us. He knows what makes us tick, what our needs are, and what is best for us in this life. No one else could possibly know as much about man as the One who created man.

Somehow many Christians today have forgotten that they were created by Jesus Christ, and they have fallen prey to the latest insights of the psychological community. For some reason, they have bought the idea that Freud, Skinner, or Rogers know more about man than Jesus does. Paul made a universal statement about our insight into man's behavior: "I do not understand what I do" (Romans 7:15). Freud doesn't understand why man does what he does. Neither do Skinner, Rogers, or anyone else.

The only One who knows the truth about man is Jesus Christ. He is the only One who understands and knows why we do what we do: "Now while He was in Jerusalem at the Passover Feast, many people saw the miraculous signs He was doing and believed in His name. But Jesus would not entrust Himself to them, for He knew all men. He did not need man's testimony about man, for He knew what was in a man" (John 2:23-25).

Second, Jesus Christ loves you and me. "For God so loved the world that He gave His one and only Son, that whoever believes in Him shall not perish but have eternal life" (John 3:16). Jesus not only knows all about us, He loves us. Someone once said this to me about their psychiatrist: Once the money stopped, so did the love and compassion. Jesus Christ is the only One who can love and accept us as we are.

This is hard to believe. In our minds we think that God must be our enemy. We try to do good, but we continue to sin and fall flat on our face. God, however, not only said that He loved us, but He also showed us that love through His Son, Jesus Christ. "But God demonstrates His own love for us in this: While we were still sinners, Christ died for us" (Romans 5:8).

And finally, Jesus Christ claims to be the solution to every need of the human heart. For everything we crave and hunger for in the depths of our souls, Jesus answers, "I AM!" He is the bread of life, the light of the world, the way, the truth, and the life; He is the resurrection and the life. He is the good shepherd who laid down His life for His sheep, and now, resurrected from the dead, cares for His sheep. If we are to find the answers to our problems, we must turn to Him.

Are you looking for answers in life? Jesus said, "Come to Me." In Him you will find rest for your soul, because in Him you will find everything you need to experience the abundant life here on earth. Are you trying to help other people with their problems? If so, be a good sheepdog. Recognize that your role is to point people back to the Shepherd.

Part 2

The Word
of God

4

Admiral Byrd

You diligently study the Scriptures because you think that by them you possess eternal life. These are the Scriptures that testify about Me, yet you refuse to come to Me to have life.

John 5:39,40

No doubt you have heard someone make the statement: "Everything is relative; there are no absolutes." And of that they are "absolutely" sure! A person who has bought into the lie that there are no absolutes will, sooner or later, exhibit the results of this belief.

Of course, most of us know there are absolutes. All of us have the need for something sure on which to lay a firm foundation and maintain stability throughout our lives. But until we come to understand this truth, our lives will remain unstable in all ways.

All scientific experimentation, for example, must start from the premise of a "constant"—something sure, unmoving, unchanging—in order to arrive at consistently accurate conclusions. Without this constant, the researcher can never be sure of his findings.

An interesting example of this need for a constant is provided by the story of Admiral Byrd's first Antarctic expedition. Byrd flew to the South Pole and there spent the six-month-long night alone. Snow after snow and blast after blast buried his small hut.

Each day he shoveled his way to the surface in order to get some exercise. There was enough light to see only a dozen yards or so as he walked the few steps he dared to take. On one such outing, having ventured as far as he dared, he turned to discover with shock that he could not see the stovepipe of his hut. Veteran that he was, the admiral controlled his tendency to panic, refusing to move because he knew the danger. To wander about without direction could place him farther from the hut.

Byrd calmly drove a stake into the snow and, using it as his center or constant, walked a large circle around it. Not finding his hut, he extended his radius and walked another circle, searching through the blackness while keeping the stake in sight. The third time he tried, the circle was so large that he almost lost sight of the stake. He returned to it—his constant—and resolved to make one more attempt, with a still larger circle.

The range of visibility was very low as he walked, holding visually to his point of reference. He knew that if he lost sight of the stake the ice and snow would quickly claim another victim. It was then that he walked squarely into the tunnel of his hut.

Byrd had relied on something sure and unchanging. And though he had groped through icy darkness, he never lost sight of his constant as it guided him to shelter and security.

The same is true of our lives. Without that constant upon which to rest our beliefs and base our judgments, we wander aimlessly, groping about in the darkness.

Some people get lost reading the Bible. It is not enough just to read the Word—you must know the living Word, Jesus Christ. The Pharisees of Jesus' day knew what the Scriptures said but didn't have a clue as to what they meant. Christ is our constant who gives us the ability to see what God's Word is saying to us.

The Bible provides a point of reference around which we must move in order to maintain stability in our lives. Whatever situation we find ourselves in, we can bounce our questions and concerns off the unchanging truth of God's Word. The lesson from Admiral Byrd holds an important secret: to keep our eyes on Christ—our constant—as we explore more of this exciting and adventurous life in Christ.

5

Jonah and the Whale

Sanctify them by the truth; Your word is truth.

John 17:17

Have you ever heard people say that they cannot believe the Bible because it contains such stories as Jonah being swallowed by a big fish, or Noah building an ark to survive the flood, or even the account of creation? "Come on!" they might say. "How do you expect me to believe the Bible when it contains so many fairy tales?" Are these stories merely fairy tales, or did they really happen? And how can we know for sure?

Trying to prove to a skeptic that Jonah was actually swallowed by a fish is an argument that is impossible to win. Even if you could prove that Jonah was in fact swallowed by a fish, would this be enough to convince a person to give his life to Christ?

The validity of the Bible is not dependent on proving that these stories are true. The validity of the Bible rests on the answer to the question, "Who is Jesus?" Jesus claimed to be God. If He is God, then we can trust what He says about the Word of God. If He is not God, then who cares if Jonah was in a fish. It will not help you or me get along better in this world today.

Since Jesus Christ is God, let's look at what Jesus said in this story:

> A wicked and adulterous generation asks for a
> miraculous sign! But none will be given it except

the sign of the prophet Jonah. For as Jonah was three days and three nights in the belly of a huge fish, so the Son of Man will be three days and three nights in the heart of the earth. The men of Nineveh will stand up at the judgment with this generation and condemn it; for they repented at the preaching of Jonah, and now one greater than Jonah is here (Matthew 12:39-41).

In this encounter with the Pharisees, Jesus clearly stated that Jonah was in the belly of a huge fish. As a matter of fact, He compared Jonah being in the belly of the fish to the fact that He would be three days and nights in the grave before He was raised from the dead.

Now if Jesus is God and He said that Jonah was in a fish, then Jonah was in a fish. I would believe the story if He said that Jonah swallowed the fish. Why? Because the validity of this story rests on the person of Jesus Christ. And if Jesus is not God, then who cares about Jonah?

The validity of the Word of God rests on the identity of Jesus Christ. All other questions raised by the skeptics concerning Jonah, Noah, and creation are merely smoke screens. In all my years of ministry, I have never encountered a person on his deathbed who wondered about Jonah. People were only interested in finding out if Jesus really was who He claimed to be, and if so, could He solve their problems.

Jesus Christ said, "Your word is truth." Because Jesus said the Word is truth, we can rest confidently in the fact the Bible holds all the answers to life's problems.

The real question we need to ask concerning God's Word is, "Who is Jesus?" Since Jesus is God, we can rest confidently in the fact that the Word is truth. We can also know that Jonah was in a fish, that Noah built an ark to survive the flood, and that the world was created in six days through God's spoken word. These events are actual history not because they can be proven scientifically, but because Jesus said they happened.

Have you settled in your mind the question, "Who is Jesus?" If not, do so today. Then you can be assured that God's Word is true. And as Jesus said, "You will know the truth, and the truth will set you free" (John 8:32).

Part 3

Forgiveness

THE DIVIDING LINE OF HUMAN HISTORY

WORLD'S PERSPECTIVE

B.C. A.D.

GOD'S PERSPECTIVE

B.C. A.D.

6

The Dividing Line of Human History

For this reason Christ is the mediator of a new covenant, that those who are called may receive the promised eternal inheritance—now that He has died as a ransom to set them free from the sins committed under the first covenant. In the case of a will, it is necessary to prove the death of the one who made it, because a will is in force only when somebody has died; it never takes effect while the one who made it is living.

Hebrews 9:15-17

It is interesting to me that the birth of Christ is the single event that divides human history into two parts. Only a small percentage of the world believes that Jesus Christ is God, that He is the Savior of the world, yet the world's calendars use Christ's birth to divide history into B.C. and A.D.—B.C. meaning "before Christ" and A.D. meaning "in the year of our Lord." Even though the world does not recognize Christ for who He is, it does recognize the fact that all of human history centers around Jesus Christ.

God, too, pointed to Jesus Christ as the centerpiece of human history. However, while we point to His birth as the dividing line, God looks at the cross of Jesus Christ as the dividing line of human history. Why? Because Jesus' death ushered in a brand-new covenant. This gives new meaning to our terminology B.C. and A.D. From God's vantage point, B.C. means "before the cross," and as I jokingly say, A.D. means "after de cross." This new covenant had been prophesied throughout the Old Testament, and the day Christ died it went into effect. It is this new covenant that we live under today.

A covenant is the same as a will. For a will or covenant to go into effect, the one who made it must die. Most of us understand this from our legal system. If you have a will, it will not go into effect until you die. This is what Hebrews 9:16,17 tells us: "In the case of a will, it is necessary to prove the death of the one who made it, because a will is in force only when somebody has died; it never takes effect while the one who made it is living." Therefore, for the new covenant that God had promised to go into effect, Christ had to die.

Now this new covenant is different than the one that God established with Moses and the nation of Israel at Mount Sinai. This old covenant was described by Paul as the "ministry of condemnation" and the "ministry that brought death" (2 Corinthians 3). It was a covenant that required man to live up to its righteous standards. To those who failed it said, "The wages of sin is death." Because man could not live up to the requirements of the old covenant, he experienced fear and guilt, and as a result could never draw near to God.

This is why God ushered in a brand-new covenant. Hebrews 8:7,8 says, "For if there had been nothing wrong with that first covenant, no place would have been sought for another. But God found fault with the people." The problem with the old covenant was us. That is why God ushered in a new covenant that is not dependent upon our abilities to live up to the law, but is totally dependent upon Jesus Christ.

Under the old covenant, the blood of bulls and goats merely covered sins. Under the new covenant, Christ's sacrifice took away our sins. Under the old covenant, sacrifices were offered again and again. Under the new covenant, Jesus died for sins once for all, and "where these have been forgiven, there is no longer any sacrifice for sin" (Hebrews 10:18). Under the old covenant, the sacrifices repeated endlessly year after year were an annual reminder of sins. Under the new covenant, God remembers our sins and lawless acts no more. Under the old covenant, the wages of sin is death. Under the new covenant, the gift of God is eternal life. Under the old covenant, it was impossible for man to draw near to God. Under the new covenant, we are encouraged to go boldly to the throne of grace calling God our Abba, Father.

Because of the cross, we are no longer under the old covenant. Today we live under the new covenant. It is a covenant based on the love and grace of God. Therefore, our acceptance before God is no longer dependent upon our self-efforts. It is totally dependent upon Christ. This is the truth that sets men free.

Are you still relating to God based on the old covenant? Or have you recognized that the cross is the dividing line of human history and that, as a result of Christ's death on the cross, we live under a brand-new covenant? Because we are under a new covenant, we have a new relationship with God our Father, and we are free to grow in love with Him and enjoy the abundant life that God has provided in the resurrected life of Jesus Christ.

7

Accounts Receivable, Accounts Payable

All this is from God, who reconciled us to Himself through Christ and gave us the ministry of reconciliation: that God was reconciling the world to Himself in Christ, not counting men's sins against them. And He has committed to us the message of reconciliation. We are therefore Christ's ambassadors, as though God were making his appeal through us. We implore you on Christ's behalf: Be reconciled to God.

2 Corinthians 5:18-20

Do you find that many Christians are not enjoying their relationship with God? Do you hear comments such as: "I know that I'm saved, but I don't feel like God likes me or accepts me" or "I'm sure He's disappointed in me"? What do you say to someone who thinks he cannot approach God?

The answer is found in the biblical truth of reconciliation. To reconcile means "to settle or resolve." That is what God has done on our behalf regarding the sin issue. He settled it once for all so that we could enjoy a relationship with Him. One of the best illustrations I know to help explain reconciliation comes from the accounting use of the word.

Let's say that you sold a piece of merchandise to a customer on credit. Thirty days pass and he fails to make a payment. Sixty days and then 90 days pass, and still no payment. Several months later you discover that the customer is bankrupt and can never pay his bill. At that point the only thing you can do is write the debt off. In other words, you reconcile the books by removing the uncollectible debt from your ledger.

What happened in this transaction? By writing the debt off your accounts receivable, you in essence paid a debt that you did not owe for a customer who owed a debt that he could not pay. This is a perfect picture of what Christ's death accomplished for us.

We owed a debt that we could not pay. The Bible declares that all men have sinned and fallen short of the glory of God (Romans 3:23). It also declares that the wages of sin is death (Romans 6:23). That is the debt we owe: death. That is what was on God's accounts receivable ledger.

God, however, reconciled His books, and in so doing reconciled us to Himself. Through Christ's death on the cross, God paid a debt that He did not owe:

> All this is from God, who reconciled us to Himself through Christ and gave us the ministry of reconciliation: that God was reconciling the world to Himself in Christ, not counting men's sins against them (2 Corinthians 5:18,19).

God has reconciled us to Himself and is not counting our sins against us because our debt has been paid in full by Jesus Christ at the cross.

> For Christ died for sins once for all, the righteous for the unrighteous, to bring you to God (1 Peter 3:18).

> He forgave us all our sins, having canceled the written code, with its regulations, that was against us and that stood opposed to us; He took it away, nailing it to the cross (Colossians 2:13,14).

> This is love: not that we loved God, but that He
> loved us and sent His Son as the One who would
> turn aside [God's] wrath, taking away our sins
> (1 John 4:10).

These verses show that Jesus Christ has done it all.

Even though Christ has done it all, we can still see ourselves as God's enemy. In Colossians, Paul writes, "Once you were alienated from God and were enemies *in your minds* because of your evil behavior" (Colossians 1:21). When we sin, it is so easy to think that God is disappointed or that He will have to punish us. This is only in our minds, however.

We may *think* that we are God's enemy, but God is not our enemy. He no longer counts our sins against us. As a matter of fact, Hebrews 10:17 states that God no longer remembers our sins and lawless acts. God has completely written off our debt. All God sees when He looks at His accounts receivable are the words "Paid in Full!"

And when He looks at us, He sees us as holy and perfect in His sight.

> But now He has reconciled you by Christ's phys-
> ical body through death to present you holy in
> His sight, without blemish and free from accusa-
> tion (Colossians 1:22).

> Because by one sacrifice He has made perfect for-
> ever those who are being made holy (Hebrews
> 10:14).

To further help us see that our reconciliation to God is complete, He tells us: "Therefore, there is now no condemnation for those who are in Christ Jesus, because through Christ Jesus the law of the Spirit of life set me free from the law of sin and death" (Romans 8:1,2).

God desires to be our friend. He paid our debt in full and removed the sin barrier that stood between us so that we could have a relationship with Him and experience the abundant life He promised. To do so, we must write the debt we owe God off our accounts payable ledger. In other words, we must believe that Christ has done it all. That is our role: to rest in the finished work of Christ.

That is why Paul writes in 2 Corinthians 5:20, "We implore you on Christ's behalf: Be reconciled to God." There is nothing left for man to do except believe: believe that God is no longer counting your sins against you, believe that God no longer remembers your sins, believe that you have been forgiven of all sins, believe that God sees you as holy and perfect, believe that there is no more condemnation for those in Christ Jesus.

Are you willing to trust Christ, and Him alone, for your own reconciliation to God? Are you willing to receive the message of God's total love, grace, and forgiveness? Are you willing to accept the plea of God to be reconciled to Him by taking the debt you owe off your accounts payable?

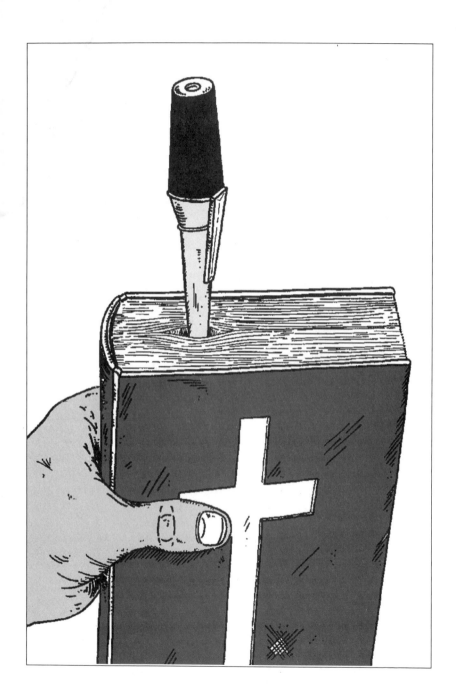

8

The Gift in a Gift

*In Him we have redemption through his blood, the forgiveness
of sins, in accordance with the riches of God's grace.*

Ephesians 1:7

Most Christians would agree that Christ lives in
them. However, when the question is asked, "Do you
believe you have total forgiveness?" many questions
arise. This is because the forgiveness of sins has often
been presented to people as a separate offer. Too many
times the gospel presentation has been, "Come down the
aisle and receive the forgiveness of sins." Certainly this is
part of the good news, but that is not all of the good
news.

Salvation is not like a vending machine, where I put
my coin in and get a little forgiveness here, a little holi-
ness there, or a little power of some sort. The gospel message is an invitation to turn to the person of Jesus Christ
by faith. And when you have received *Him*, you have
received *everything*.

To get a better understanding of this, let's say I held a
pen in one hand and a Bible in the other. Let the pen represent forgiveness and the Bible represent Christ. I then
place the pen within the open pages and close the Bible.
Where is the pen? Obviously, it is in the Bible. Now if the
pen represents forgiveness and the Bible represents
Christ, where is forgiveness found? It is found in Christ.

It is impossible to have one without the other. If I were to hand you the Bible, you would have the pen as well. But you might say, "All I want is the pen." You can't have the pen apart from the book. It is a two-for-one deal.

So it is with forgiveness. The issue in salvation is Christ—not what He can do for you, but His offering His very life to you. The moment we receive Christ, we receive His total forgiveness because forgiveness is in Him. That's why Ephesians 1:7 says, "In Him we have... forgiveness of sins." All that God has to offer us is in His Son, Jesus Christ.

To believe that Christ lives in you and still doubt your total forgiveness is a contradiction. Jesus Christ could never live in a person unless all of his sins were forgiven. He died *for* you so that He could live *in* you! His life in us is our assurance that we are totally forgiven and secure in that salvation.

It is impossible to receive Christ without receiving forgiveness of sins. It would be like offering you the pen separate from the Bible. If you are struggling with your forgiveness, ask yourself if you are in Christ. If you are in Christ, you can rest confidently in the fact that you have forgiveness of sins.

9

The Two-Sided Coin of Salvation

God made Him who had no sin to be sin for us,
so that in Him we might become the righteousness of God.

2 Corinthians 5:21

Salvation is like a coin. It has two sides. On one side is forgiveness, and on the other is righteousness. On one side, God provided total forgiveness of our sins in Christ. On the other side, and equally as important, He gave to us His very righteousness. Both transactions make up the coin of salvation.

Many of us, however, view salvation only from the forgiveness side of the coin. It never enters our minds to turn the coin over to see what is on the other side. Somehow, we have the idea that if we could just get all our sins forgiven, we would be wonderful people.

This idea is not true. Having our sins forgiven does not make us righteous. We could quit sinning altogether and still not be righteous in God's sight. Righteousness (a right standing of total acceptability before God) is a gift that must be given to us.

The Bible declares, "There is no one righteous, not even one" (Romans 3:10). We have no righteousness of our own, and there is no way to become righteous by being good enough or by living up to God's righteous standards. Romans 3:20 says that "no one will be declared righteous in His sight by observing the law." So for us to be righteous in God's sight, we have to be made righteous.

Before we could be made righteous, however, we had to be cleansed of all our unrighteousness. That is the forgiveness side of the coin of salvation and is what Christ did for us at the cross. First John 1:9 says, "If we confess our sins, He is faithful and just and will forgive us our sins and purify us from all unrighteousness." Jesus Christ went to the cross 2000 years ago and died for all our sins one time. And in so doing, He cleansed us from all our unrighteousness.

God, however, did not simply take our sins and place them on Jesus. He also took Christ's perfect righteousness and gave it to us through His resurrected life—the other side of the coin of salvation. Second Corinthians 5:21 says, "God made Him who had no sin to be sin for us, so that in Him we might become the righteousness of God." In Christ we have been given the very righteousness of God. As a result, we are as righteous and acceptable in the sight of God as Jesus Christ!

We aren't righteous in God's sight because of what we have done. We are righteous because we have received the righteous One. His righteousness is a free gift to us when we receive Him by faith. Romans 5:17 puts it this way: "For if, by the trespass of the one man, death reigned through that one man, how much more will those who receive God's abundant provision of grace and of the *gift of righteousness* reign in life through the one man, Jesus Christ." This may sound too good to be true, but it is the truth.

Righteousness is a gift. No one can work for it or earn it. And no one deserves to be made righteous. Like any gift, righteousness can only be accepted or rejected. Once a person has accepted Jesus Christ, he or she has accepted His gift of righteousness and can say, "I am as righteous as Jesus Christ."

Salvation—a two-sided coin. On one side is forgiveness; on the other is the righteousness of Christ. If you are in Christ, you are totally forgiven through Christ's death on the cross. And equally important, you have been given the righteousness of Christ through His resurrected life.

Today you can stand before God confident that you are totally acceptable in His sight—not because of what you have done, but because of what Christ has done on your behalf.

10

My Dad, the Judge

*He did it to demonstrate His justice at the present time,
so as to be just and the One who justifies the man
who has faith in Jesus.*

Romans 3:26

An often-asked question is, "How can God be both just and loving at the same time?" For Him to be both seems like a contradiction to our finite minds. If He is loving, it seems He would have to compromise His justice. If He is just, then it seems He would have to withdraw His love.

In the cross, however, we see these two seemingly contradictory characteristics come together. In Romans, Paul describes Christ's death on the cross as both a demonstration of God's justice (Romans 3:26) and a demonstration of God's love (Romans 5:8). It is much like the following illustration of the judge.

A young man was arrested for a crime. During the trial all the evidence was presented to determine this young man's guilt or innocence. The evidence was clear. The judge slammed down his gavel and said, "Guilty as charged!" Then he set the maximum fine of one million dollars for punishment.

An amazing thing happened, however. The judge slipped off his robe, stepped down from his bench, and paid the fine. Why? The judge was more than a judge. He was the young man's father. And his love for his son was so great that he was willing to pay the penalty for his son's crime.

In so doing, the punishment for the crime had been executed, justice had been served, and the young man was free to go. The judge was both just and loving. As a just judge, he could not simply dismiss the crime. Otherwise, the law would have been compromised. As a loving father he paid the penalty so that his son could go free.

That is exactly what Jesus Christ did for you and me. As our judge, He declared, "All have sinned and fall short of the glory of God" (Romans 3:23). His verdict is "guilty," and the punishment is death—"For the wages of sin is death" (Romans 6:23). Jesus Christ is more than our judge. He is our heavenly Father. As our Father, He took off His judicial robe and went to a cross on our behalf to pay the penalty for all our sins.

Jesus Christ did not compromise His justice. Our sin did not go unpunished. His death on the cross paid in full the penalty for all our sins. Justice has been executed. Nor did He withdraw His love. As John writes, "Greater love has no one than this, that one lay down his life for his friends" (John 15:13). Jesus Christ laid down His life for us so that we could experience new life in Him.

Jesus Christ is just and loving. He demonstrated both through His death on the cross. If you are not experiencing the love of God, it is because you have not fully understood the justice of God. Recognize that all of your sins have been judged and the punishment has been executed. Christ took it all. When you do, you will start the great adventure of growing in the love of God.

CLEANSED
AT THE CROSS

FILLED

SEALED
BY THE PROMISED HOLY SPIRIT

11

Cleansed, Filled, and Sealed

To them God has chosen to make known among
the Gentiles the glorious riches of this mystery,
which is Christ in you, the hope of glory.

Colossians 1:27

In counseling sessions, both in person and on the radio broadcast of "People to People," or wherever I encounter a Christian who is struggling, I ask the question, "What is your understanding of salvation?" In almost every instance, the answer comes back, "Jesus died for my sins so I can go to heaven when I die."

Although this answer is partially right, it falls far short of the total salvation God provided for us in Jesus Christ. Salvation is much more than forgiveness of sins; it is the imputation of life—*Christ's* life. Jesus did not come simply to get men out of hell and into heaven. His ultimate goal was to get Himself out of heaven and back into men.

Canning is an illustration that paints a perfect picture of salvation. Many of you ladies have done some canning. What's the first thing you do when you begin the canning process? You sterilize the jars, don't you?

Now, why do you sterilize the jars? Is it just to have a bunch of nice, clean, sterilized jars sitting around? What if your husband comes home while you are sterilizing jars and asks, "What are you doing, honey?"

"Oh, sterilizing jars."

"What are you doing that for?"

"Just to have some clean jars."

"What are you going to do tomorrow?"

"Sterilize more jars."

"Well, what are you going to do with those jars?"

"Keep 'em clean. Any time they get a speck of dirt in them, I'm gonna stick 'em under the water and get 'em clean again. I have sterilized them and I am going to keep 'em that way."

"What are you going to do the next day?"

"Keep 'em clean—just keep those jars clean." Your husband would think that you had lost your mind. You don't sterilize jars just to have a bunch of clean jars sitting around.

You sterilize the jars because you are planning on putting food in them. And if the jars are not totally cleansed of all impurities and you put food in them, what happens to the food? It spoils. The reason for sterilizing the jars is so the food will not spoil or rot.

That is what happened 2000 years ago at the cross. God cleansed our jar of all unrighteousness. Why? So that He could have a bunch of cleansed vessels down here on earth? No! He cleansed us of all unrighteousness so that His life could fill us "without spoiling." That is what salvation is: the imputation of life. We have been cleansed once for all so that we could be filled with the very life of Christ. That is why Paul describes salvation in Colossians 1:27 as "Christ in you, the hope of glory."

It is interesting that once food is placed in the jar, the jar is described by what's in it. For example, if you put applesauce in the jar, it becomes a jar of applesauce. The identity of the jar is determined by what's in it. So it is with us. When Christ comes to live in us, we become children of God.

Once the jar has been filled with food, something else happens. The jar is then sealed. Sealing the jar is what keeps the good things in and the bad things that would spoil the food out. It is the final step in the canning process.

After we have been filled with the life of Christ, we too are sealed. Ephesians 1:13 (NASB) tells us, "In Him, you also, after listening to the message of truth, the gospel of your salvation—having also believed, you were sealed in Him with the Holy Spirit of promise." The Holy Spirit is the guarantee of our salvation. Knowing that we have been sealed enables us to walk confidently in God's promise: "Never will I leave you; never will I forsake you" (Hebrews 13:5).

Cleansing, filling, and sealing—a wonderful picture of salvation. It helps us to see that salvation is much more than forgiveness of sins. Jesus Christ cleansed us once for all 2000 years ago so that He could fill us with His life today. And once Christ has come to live in our hearts, He seals us with the promised Holy Spirit. Salvation, then, can be summed up in this statement: Jesus Christ gave His life for you, so that He could give His life to you, so that He could live His life through you.

What is important in canning is what is placed in the jar. Once it was just a jar. Now it is a jar of applesauce. What is important about salvation is that Christ has come to live in our hearts. Once we were just children. Now we are children of God. When we see that this is the true goal of salvation, the cross of Jesus Christ where we have been cleansed once for all takes on a whole new meaning.

I have seen literally thousands of Christians stop struggling in their experience once they understood that salvation is more than forgiveness of sins. If you are struggling in your Christian life, maybe it is because you have never gone beyond the forgiveness issue to see that salvation is life.

If this is the case in your life, will you by faith accept that Christ's death cleansed you of all unrighteousness and that now the risen Christ wants to come and live His life in and through you? Once you see that completeness of salvation, you will no longer have to struggle trying to keep your jar cleansed. Now you can go on to enjoy the life of Christ living in you.

You have been cleansed, filled, and sealed. The transaction is complete. Therefore, enjoy the abundant life that God has promised.

Part
4

Life

12

Bridging the Gap

I tell you the truth, whoever hears My word and
believes Him who sent Me has eternal life and will not be
condemned; he has crossed over from death to life.

John 5:24

For the longest time my explanation of the gospel
centered solely around the forgiveness issue. If you had
asked me as a Christian how I was saved, I would have
answered, "Through Christ's death on the cross." I have
asked the question, "What does it mean to be saved?" of
other people. In most cases the answer is, "Jesus died for
my sins and there will be a place for me in heaven when
I die." I have used an illustration based on the forgiveness issue to help explain salvation. The illustration
shows a man standing at the side of a cliff, overlooking a
deep chasm with God on the other side. In the illustration, the cross of Jesus is what bridges the gap and
enables us to experience God's forgiveness. In the last
several years, however, I have discovered that the gospel
is more than forgiveness. Now my illustration has taken
on a new meaning.

From the time I received Christ, Romans has been
one of my favorite books of the Bible. I have read it
dozens of times. While reading through Romans on one
occasion, Romans 5:10 jumped out at me as if I had never
seen it before. It reads, "For if, when we were God's enemies, we were reconciled to Him through the death of

His Son, how much more, having been reconciled, shall we be saved through His life!" I read this verse and asked, "What did life have to do with anything?"

Jesus Christ not only died for our sins but was raised again from the dead. I knew what the cross of Jesus Christ meant, but I had no idea of the significance of His resurrection. Sometimes we are absolute geniuses at overlooking the obvious. What is the most obvious implication of the word "resurrection"? The restoration of life!

Perhaps you have had the experience of having a word called to your attention for the first time. Suddenly you begin finding that word again while reading the newspaper, in conversations, and on billboards—seemingly behind every bush. You know, of course, that the word was there all the time; you were just unconscious of it. That was my experience with the word "life" in the Bible. Suddenly it was everywhere. It seemed as if God had snuck in and rewritten the Bible when I wasn't looking.

Seeing the word "life" throughout the Scriptures brought to mind other Scripture references. For example, Ephesians 2:1: "As for you, you were dead in your transgressions and sins." This verse made me ask the question, "What kind of person needs life?" The answer was obvious: only the dead. Before if I was asked what the problem of mankind is, I would have always discussed man's sinfulness and the need for God's forgiveness. This is certainly true, but man's problem is much deeper. From God's point of view, the problem of man is not just that he is a sinner, but that he is dead and in need of life.

This brings us back to our illustration of how to explain the gospel. Man is not only standing at the edge of the chasm in his sins, but he is standing there also spiritually dead and in need of life. And the only spiritual life that is available for man is the life of God.

Before God could give man spiritual life, however, He had to deal with the thing that killed man in the first place. When Adam came into the world, he was created alive spiritually. God told him he could eat from all the trees in the garden except for one, and that was the tree of the knowledge of good and evil. God told Adam that the day he ate the fruit of this tree, he would surely die. Through the temptation of Satan, Adam and Eve ate of the tree of the knowledge of good and evil. But they did not die physically that day. The Bible records that they lived to be over 900 years old. How did they die then? They died spiritually. They were separated from the life of Christ. That is what death is: the absence of life.

Adam passed sin on to all of mankind. As it says in Romans 5:12, "Therefore, just as sin entered the world through one man, and death through sin, and in this way death came to all men, because all sinned." Every man and woman born into this world is born in the same condition that Adam was in after he sinned: spiritually dead. What killed mankind? *Sin!* So before God could restore back to us what we had lost in Adam, He had to deal with what killed us: sin.

Two thousand years ago Jesus Christ went to a cross and took upon Himself all of our sins. There He paid a debt He did not owe for us who owed a debt we could not pay. Through His death Jesus took away the sins of the entire world, and as a result there is absolutely nothing that can keep us separated from the life of God except our refusal to accept His life through Jesus Christ. We receive the life of Christ today by faith. When we simply put our trust in Jesus Christ—the fact that He died and was raised from the dead—He comes to live in us through the Holy Spirit. Jesus Christ laid down His life for us, so that He could give His life to us, so that He could live His life through us. That is the gospel. Man stands dead in His sins, separated from the life of God.

God reaches across to man through His Son, Jesus Christ, offering us the very life that raised Jesus from the dead.

Have you recognized that the gap has been bridged in the person of Jesus Christ, and that all of your sins have been taken away through Christ's death 2000 years ago? Have you recognized that you are dead in your sins and that the only thing a dead man needs is life? If so, are you willing to accept into your heart the same life that raised Jesus from the dead? Realize that the gospel is more than forgiveness of sins. As John 5:24 puts it, "Whoever hears My word and believes Him who sent me has eternal life and will not be condemned; he has crossed over from death to life." It is through the resurrection of Jesus Christ that any man, woman, boy, or girl on the face of the earth who comes to Him in faith receives His very life through the indwelling Holy Spirit. That is how we live!

13

How to Save a Drowning Man

Now there were many of those priests, since death prevented them from continuing in office; but because Jesus lives forever, He has a permanent priesthood. Therefore He is able to save completely those who come to God through Him, because He always lives to intercede for them.

Hebrews 7:23-25

God chose to give you and me eternal life. He could have given us temporary life or some other type of life. He chose, however, to give us eternal life. And this eternal life is in His Son, Jesus Christ. John writes:

> And this is the testimony: God has given us eternal life, and this life is in His Son. He who has the Son has life; he who does not have the Son of God does not have life. I write these things to you who believe in the name of the Son of God so that you may know that you have eternal life (1 John 5:11-13).

Are you in Christ? Is He in you? Then what kind of life do you have? Eternal life! When does this eternal life begin? The minute that you have the Son. How long is this life going to last? Forever! It is eternal life because it is His life. How long is Christ going to live? Forever!

Therefore, how long are you going to live if you have the Son?

Many people, however, perceive salvation along a different line. Let me illustrate. Suppose you are motoring along in your boat and see a guy out in the water drowning. Someone says, "Hey, that guy needs to be saved."

You respond, "That's obvious, but how do you go about saving him?"

"Oh, by your good example."

So, you jump out of the boat and say, "Watch me swim." As you are demonstrating how to swim, you look over and see the guy going under. "Obviously," you say to yourself, "you can't save someone by a good example."

Somebody else says, "You can save the guy through education."

This sounds good. So you find a book on how to swim and throw it to the guy out in the water. "Just read this," you shout from the boat. "It will teach you how to swim." As the guy in the water makes an attempt to reach the book, he goes under the water again. Education certainly isn't the answer.

Another person says, "Grab the guy out of the water, and put him in your boat. That will save him."

Of all the suggestions you have heard, this one makes the most sense. So you paddle over to the drowning guy. Then you reach out, grab him and pull him in the boat. With a big sigh, you say, "Whew, I finally saved him." But is this salvation?

Not really, because as you are paddling to shore, the guy asks you for a cigarette. This makes you mad. You think to yourself, "This ungrateful slob. I saved his life and all he wants to do is smoke a cigarette. One more like that and back in the water he goes."

Then he says a cuss word. As a matter of fact, he starts cussing at you for not saving him sooner. This really makes you mad. So you pitch him right back in the water to drown.

Now was this salvation? Was the rescue complete? No, it was merely a temporary reprieve. This is what so many people think concerning salvation—that they might do something to make God so mad that He will pitch them right out of the boat. It's as if they think John 3:16 reads like this: "For God so loved the world that He gave His one and only Son, that whoever believes in Him shall not perish but have *a temporary reprieve.*" Salvation is much more, however.

Salvation is when you grab the guy out of the water, put him in your boat, and then deliver him safely to shore. Anything short of that is a disgrace to what God called eternal life.

When God saved you, He grabbed you out of the water and delivered you safely to shore. He saved you completely. He did not give you a temporary reprieve. He gave you His life, and His life is eternal. That is what salvation is—the imputation of life. Colossians 2:13 says: "When you were dead in your sins and in the uncircum- cision of your sinful nature, God made you alive with Christ."

He didn't give you life because you were a neat person. Nor does He remain in you and you in Him because you act good. He saves you completely and delivers you safely to shore because He is faithful. As Hebrews 7:25 states: "He is able to save completely those who come to God through Him."

John said he wrote his letter so we would *know* that we have eternal life. He didn't say, "I write these things to you who believe in the name of the Son of God so that you may *hope* that you have eternal life." If you have the Son, you can know with confidence that you have eternal

life. And because eternal life is something you did not earn, it is something you can never lose.

Do you know that you have eternal life? Do you have the Son? If so, you can know that God has saved you completely. He will never throw you back in the water. Eternal life is yours to experience forever!

14

At the End of
My Rope

*But we have this treasure in jars of clay to show that
this all-surpassing power is from God and not from us.*

2 Corinthians 4:7

Have you ever found yourself in a situation where
you almost felt like giving up? You may have tried everything in your ability to better the situation, but no matter
how hard you tried, it seemed to just get worse. You
probably felt like you were at the end of your rope.

I have heard this many times in counseling situations. I will talk to people who say, "I am almost at the
end of my rope!" My response to someone who makes
this statement is, "Put some grease on that thing so you
can get to the end of it." This may not sound very sympa-
thetic at first, but the truth is, that's exactly where God
wants us to be. The only way we can experience His
strength and sufficiency is when we stop trusting in our
own.

Quite often we find ourselves in trying situations in
our relationships with other people. It may be a boss who
is not a Christian, an overbearing in-law, or a child who
is a bit too active. Whatever the circumstance, our
patience runs thin and we begin to get angry and bitter.
We usually respond with, "Lord, just give me strength to

endure this!" What we need to understand is that God doesn't want to help us with our patience or ability. He sent His Son so we could die to ourselves and trust *His* ability.

You can hold onto your own intellectual understanding or willpower. But sooner or later, given the right circumstances, these things are going to give out. You can either "let go of your rope" and trust Christ to work in and through you in the midst of the situation, or you can continue to hold on to your own resources, just hanging there, never experiencing true joy and freedom.

Paul wrote in 2 Corinthians 12:10: "I delight in weaknesses, in insults, in hardships, in persecutions, in difficulties. For when I am weak, then I am strong." In the midst of our day-to-day hardships and struggles, we can experience the peace and the strength of Christ.

Are you still hanging on to your rope? Are you still clinging to your own understanding and ability? If so, let go and allow the Lord to take control of your circumstance. That is why He sent His Son, who was without sin, to die in our place. Christ took the penalty for our sin so that, raised from the dead, He could live His life in us. He is the only one who *can* live the Christian life. All He expects from us is simply to trust Him—to let go and let Him guide and direct us.

Part

5

Identity

15

Alone on a Deserted Island

Yet to all who received Him, to those who believed in His name, He gave the right to become children of God.

John 1:12

The issue of identity is inescapable and central to our lives. We all ask, "Who am I?" Tied in with this drive for identity are the spiritual needs of unconditional love and acceptance, and a meaning and purpose to life. That is why so much of our time and energy is devoted to discovering who we are. Since this need for identity is so strong, how do we determine who we are?

Imagine yourself for a moment living on a deserted island without ever having seen another human being. It's just you and the coconut tree. Suddenly a voice comes out of heaven and asks, "Who are you?" You wouldn't have the slightest idea how to answer.

Then a ship appears on the horizon and arrives at the island. A man splashes to shore. He runs to you, embraces you, and shouts, "At last! I have found my long-lost child!"

"Who are you?" you ask.

"I'm John Doe. And you are my son, Pat."

Again the voice from heaven asks, "Who are you?"

Now you know the answer. "I'm Pat Doe. John Doe's son."

As this illustration points out, a person's identity is determined by his relationship to someone or something. We so desperately want to know who we are that we will latch on to practically anything. We determine our identities through our appearance, occupation, abilities, family relationships, friends, denominational affiliation, and many other ways. The common denominator of all these human attempts to find identity is that they are all temporal. They can change with the wind.

Suppose that you have determined your identity by your profession. "I'm a businessman," you say. What happens if you get fired or retire? Who are you then? As a matter of fact, statistics show that a large percentage of men die within two years of their retirement. Why? Because they no longer know who they are. Suppose a person determines his identity through the role he fulfills. A woman might say, "I'm a mother." That is her identity. What happens when the kids leave home? Who is she then?

There is only one identity that cannot be shaken, one foundation that cannot be taken away from you: "I'm a child of God." Now you might be a child of God who works in the business world, or practices medicine, or plays a sport, or serves as a mother. But your true identity comes from your relationship with your God and Father. And knowing that you are a child of God is the only way to experience true security in this world.

As our illustration showed, our identity comes from who we are identified with. When you were born into this world, you were totally identified with Adam. You were a lost sinner, dead and in need of life. That was your identity. Our identity can be changed, however, through faith in Jesus Christ. When we come to Christ by faith, God gives us a brand-new identity: "Yet to all who received Him, to those who believed in His name, He gave the right to become children of God" (John 1:12).

As children of God, we can experience a personal relationship with God as our Father. Paul wrote in Galatians 4:6: "Because you are sons, God sent the Spirit of His Son into our hearts, the Spirit who calls out, 'Abba, Father.'" "Abba" is the most intimate of Hebrew terms. It is similar to our word "Daddy." We can come to God calling Him "Daddy, Father."

No longer do we need to live in fear of God. As Romans 8:15 puts it, "You did not receive a spirit that makes you a slave again to fear, but you received the Spirit of sonship." And "the Spirit Himself testifies with our spirit that we are God's children" (Romans 8:16). No matter what circumstance we may be in, God's Spirit testifies to our spirit that we are His children. Knowing this enables us to approach God with confidence in our time of need.

The believer's identity in Christ is not a side issue; it is central to experiencing the real Christian life. If we do not have a firm grip on who we are, we will not have the confidence to go to our God and Father for help when we need it the most.

If a voice came out of heaven and asked you, "Who are you?" what would you say? I hope that you would respond with confidence, "I'm a child of God!"

16

Caterpillars and Butterflies

Therefore, if anyone is in Christ, he is a new creation; the old has gone, the new has come!

2 Corinthians 5:17

What does it mean to be a new creature in Christ? Does it mean that we used to drink, smoke, or do some other sin, and now we don't? Or does it mean something else?

Jesus told Nicodemus what it meant to become a new creature when He said, "You must be born again" (John 3:7). To be made into a new creature is to be born of the Spirit of God. It is much like a caterpillar becoming a butterfly.

Initially, a caterpillar is a hairy, ugly, earthbound creature. You can try to change the caterpillar by dressing it up, making it smell nice, or even educating it at Caterpillar University, but it is still a caterpillar. For the caterpillar to change, it must go through the process of metamorphosis.

When it does, the caterpillar weaves a cocoon and is totally immersed in it. Within the cocoon, the process of metamorphosis takes place. Finally a brand-new creature emerges called a butterfly. Once ground-bound, the butterfly can now soar through the sky.

In the same way, when you and I were born into this world, we were born under the law of sin and death. The Bible tells us that we are all sinners, separated from the life of God. We, too, try to look good, smell good, educate ourselves to act good, but underneath we are still sinners. For us to be made new, we must be born again.

We are born again through placing our faith in Jesus Christ. The Bible describes the changes that take place this way: "When you were *dead* in your sins and in the uncircumcision of your flesh, God made you *alive* with Christ" (Colossians 2:13). We pass from death to life and emerge a brand-new creature with Christ living in us. "I have been crucified with Christ and I no longer live, but *Christ lives in me*. The life I live in the body, I live by faith in the Son of God, who loved me and gave Himself for me" (Galatians 2:20).

We are new creatures because Christ lives in us. This means that we have the mind of Christ (1 Corinthians 2:16), and therefore have the ability to see life from God's perspective rather than man's perspective.

As new creatures in Christ, we may not always act like new creatures in Christ. Sometimes we might land on things we shouldn't, or forget that we are butterflies and crawl around with our old worm buddies. The truth, however, is that once we are new creatures in Christ we will never be old sinners again!

It would never occur to you to call a butterfly a "good-looking converted worm." Why not? After all, it was a worm, and it was "converted." It is now a new creature, and you don't think of it in terms of what it was. We, too, were once old sinners and were converted, but that is not what we are today.

That is why Paul addresses all of his letters to the "saints" and not to all the "old sinners saved by grace." Being a new creature in Christ means that we have a brand-new identity. And this new identity is not determined by how we act. Once again, we are new creatures because Christ lives in us. Our role is merely to see ourselves from God's perspective.

When we sin today, it is like the Lord brings a huge mirror and places it above us and asks, "Who are you?"

You look up and say, "A butterfly, Lord."

"Then why are you crawling around with the worms?"

"I don't know, Lord. It doesn't make much sense, does it?"

And then it's as if the Lord says, "I didn't make you into a new creature so that you could crawl around like a worm. I made you into a new creature so that you could fly with the butterflies. Get up and fly!"

Our new identity is now the motivation for our behavior. Paul tells us in Ephesians 5:8, "You were once darkness, but now you are light in the Lord. Live as children of light." A good paraphrase is "Once you were a worm; now you are a butterfly. Fly like a butterfly!" It just makes sense.

If you have come to Christ by faith, you are a brand-new creature—a saint in the sight of God. Christ lives in you. You don't have to pretend to be a new creature or try to act like a butterfly. This is who you are. Recognize it and begin trusting Christ to live His life through you.

17

You're Rich

*Praise be to the God and Father of our Lord Jesus Christ,
who has blessed us in the heavenly realms
with every spiritual blessing in Christ.*

Ephesians 1:3

Why is the average Christian not experiencing freedom in Christ in his daily life? It is directly related to his lack of understanding of the riches we have in Christ Jesus.

One of the greatest illustrations of the importance of spiritual knowledge is the true story of a man named Yates. During the depression years, Mr. Yates owned a lot of undeveloped land in west Texas. He raised sheep to earn a living. Like most people during the depression, Mr. Yates lived in extreme poverty, struggling just to feed and clothe his family.

His situation worsened to the point that he couldn't pay even the small amount of taxes due on the land. He was in danger of losing his property altogether. As Mr. Yates was facing inevitable bankruptcy, an oil company approached him. "We think there may be oil on your property. Will you allow us to drill?" Reasoning that he had little to lose, Mr. Yates gave them permission.

The oil company began drilling immediately. At a very shallow depth, they struck the largest oil deposit at that time on the North American continent—a deposit which produced 80,000 barrels of oil every day! Overnight, Mr. Yates became a billionaire!

Or did he? If you think about it, Mr. Yates had been a billionaire ever since he first signed the papers to acquire the land. The oil was always there. Mr. Yates just didn't know it.

There are many Christians today who are living in the identical situation spiritually. The Bible tells us that God "has blessed us in the heavenly realms with every spiritual blessing in Christ" (Ephesians 1:3).

However, like Mr. Yates, most of us are unaware of the incredible riches that we already have in Christ. We live our lives in spiritual poverty, struggling day to day, not experiencing the life and freedom He has provided.

But it doesn't have to be that way. There is oil on our property. God has provided an eternal inheritance for us, His children. In Christ we have riches far greater than those of Mr. Yates! The day we came to the Lord Jesus Christ in saving faith, God gave us everything we would ever need "for life and godliness through our knowledge of Him" (2 Peter 1:3).

The apostle Paul prayed in Ephesians that the "eyes of our hearts" would be opened. Head knowledge is not enough; we need a true heart knowledge of God and the riches of His love and grace that are ours in Christ Jesus. Are the "eyes of your heart" open to see what God has freely given you?

Part

6

Law and Grace

18

Don't Get Stuck in the Desert

There remains, then, a Sabbath-rest for the people of God;
for anyone who enters God's rest also rests
from his own work, just as God did from His.

Hebrews 4:9,10

Does this picture look familiar to you? It is a perfect picture of my life. When I accepted Christ over 20 years ago, my desire was to be "God's guy." Whatever He desired for me, whatever He wanted me to do, that is what I desired. People I looked up to told me that in order to be God's guy, I needed to witness, to pray, to memorize Scripture, to be involved in a local church. So off I went to get involved in every Christian activity possible.

I quickly became a "go-go" Christian, doing all the "right things," and at first loving every minute of it. But after several years, things changed. Instead of feeling like God's guy, I felt like I was racing madly on a spiritual treadmill. I was highly active but going nowhere. What a contrast my life was to the "Sabbath-rest" that is talked about in the book of Hebrews.

My life reminded me of the story of Israel after Moses led them through the Red Sea. It was never God's intention that the Israelites linger in the desert. He told them to go straight to the Promised Land, where they could eat from trees they did not plant and drink from wells they did not dig. But because of their unbelief, they did not enter into the rest to which God had called them. Afraid to go ahead and unable to return to Egypt, the desert was all they had left, with its boredom, monotony, and dryness.

Being engaged in so many activities, I lost the joy that I had experienced when I first came to know the Lord. Every now and then a small voice in my heart would ask, "Is this really what the Lord Jesus had in mind when He talked about an 'abundant life'?" Like the Israelites, I had a choice: I could either enter the Sabbath-rest God called me to—resting totally in the truth of His unconditional love and grace—or live in the desert. For almost eight years of my Christian life, I settled for second best.

God has prepared for you and me a Promised Land called a Sabbath-rest. Our rest is not found in a land but in our relationship with the living Christ. God has always had a remnant of people who have said, "Lord, I'm not satisfied with the same old thing. I don't want to practice a religion; I want to know You in a real relationship." The hungry ones, the humble ones, God will always lead into the Sabbath-rest.

This rest is described in Hebrews 4:9,10: "There remains, then, a Sabbath-rest for the people of God; for anyone who enters God's rest also rests from his own work, just as God did from His." God wants us to grasp by faith the fact that Jesus has done it all, and there is nothing left for us to perform to be acceptable to God. In other words, "God has done the work; now you rest!"

This "resting" is not the same thing as being inactive. I can't think of anyone more active than Jesus Christ. Just as Christ rested in the fact that it was His Father doing His work through Him (John 14:10), so we too can rest in the truth that it is Christ living His life, doing His work through us. When we make ourselves available to God, we will be more active than ever, but the work will be Christ's.

Are you roaming in the desert of spiritual activity, trying to make yourself acceptable to God? God has something better for you. It is called the Sabbath-rest. Don't settle for second best like the Israelites did, and like I did for eight years. Enter God's rest. Rest from your works, just as He has rested from His.

19

The Old and the New Don't Mix

Neither do men pour new wine into old wineskins.
If they do, the skins will burst, the wine will run out
and the wineskins will be ruined. No, they pour new wine
into new wineskins, and both are preserved.

Matthew 9:17

Have you ever heard this statement: "God's grace gives us the ability to live up to God's law"? This attitude is prevalent among Christians today. We recognize that we are saved by grace. We would even call someone a heretic who said otherwise. But when it comes to living the Christian life, we think that is done through obedience to the law. What we are doing is mingling law and grace.

This is not a new problem. Paul addressed it throughout his letters, and primarily in the book of Galatians. As a matter of fact, the mixing of law and grace is commonly referred to as "Galatianism." Jesus addressed this issue and showed the damage it causes in His illustration of pouring new wine into old wineskins.

Some of Jesus' critics asked Him why His disciples were not observing all the legalistic traditions that had been passed down. Specifically, they wanted to know why His disciples were not fasting. He responded: "Neither do men pour new wine into old wineskins. If they do, the skins will burst, the wine will run out and the wineskins will be ruined. No, they pour new wine into new wineskins, and both are preserved" (Matthew 9:17).

In the wine-making process in Jesus' day, after the grapes had been picked and the juice squeezed out of them, it was poured into a new wineskin. In the wineskin, this new wine fermented, producing a gas that expanded and stretched the wineskin to its capacity. Once the skin had been stretched, it was never used again.

If it was, the new wine would stretch the old wineskin beyond its capacity. The wineskin would burst, and you would lose both the wine and the wineskin. That is what we do when we mix law and grace; we ruin the purpose of each. We rob the law of its terror and condemnation, and rob grace of its freedom, joy, and life.

It is important for us to realize the major division in the Bible is that between law and grace. This division is seen in John 1:17: "For the law was given through Moses; grace and truth came through Jesus Christ." And what was given through Moses (law) has a totally separate and distinct purpose from that which came through Jesus Christ (grace and truth).

The law was given to Moses at Mount Sinai after the Israelites crossed through the Red Sea to escape their bondage in Egypt. God gave the law to Israel for their protection. This law, however, has a purpose in our lives on a spiritual level. Paul writes throughout his letters that the purpose of the law is to convict us of our need for salvation and then point us to Jesus Christ so that we might have salvation in Him. This makes sense. Why would we ever turn to Christ for salvation if we didn't know that we needed salvation?

So the law does its work by pointing out our sinfulness (Romans 3:20); by showing us that apart from Christ we are dead in our sins (Romans 7:9,10); and then, as

Galatians 3:24 states: "The law was put in charge to lead us to Christ that we might be justified by faith." That is the purpose of the law. And once the law has done its work, Galatians 3:25 says, "Now that faith has come, we are no longer under the supervision of the law."

Paul could not have made this point any clearer: The law has no place in the believer's life. Paul amplifies this in Romans 6:14 where he says, "You are not under law, but under grace." As Christians, we live under the grace of God—the grace that came through Christ Jesus.

God did not intend for us to try to live up to the standards of the law. He knew that was an impossibility for us. In our pride, however, we think that we can keep the law. Because we can't, the law continues to condemn us by showing us our sinfulness. That is what Paul meant when he said in Galatians 2:18, "If I rebuild what I destroyed, I prove that I am a lawbreaker." The law condemns us before salvation. And if we try to live up to it as a Christian, it continues to condemn us. That is the law's purpose.

It is no wonder so many Christians live defeated lives. They are trying to live up to something that was meant to condemn and kill them. If we are going to experience the abundant life that Jesus promised, then we must die to the law and come alive to the grace of God.

The same grace that saves us is what sustains us in our Christian life. Paul learned that God's grace is enough. In 2 Corinthians 12:9, God told him, "My grace is sufficient for you." God's grace gives us life (Ephesians 2:4,5), enables us to go through trials and tribulations, and teaches us to say no to unrighteousness and "live self-controlled, upright and godly lives in this present age" (Titus 2:12). It only takes a little bit of the law, however, to ruin God's purpose in grace. You cannot mix the two. The new wine of grace cannot be contained in the old wineskin of law.

These are the words Paul had for those who mingled law and grace:

> You foolish Galatians! Who has bewitched you? Before your very eyes Jesus Christ was clearly portrayed as crucified. I would like to learn just one thing from you: Did you receive the Spirit by observing the law, or by believing what you heard? Are you so foolish? After beginning with the Spirit, are you now trying to attain your goal by human effort? (Galatians 3:1-3).

Like the Galatians, are you trying to live the Christian life through self-effort? If so, are you willing to recognize that the law has done its work in your life—that it has pointed out your sinfulness and your need for Christ? Are you willing to recognize that as a child of God you are no longer under the law, but under the grace of God?

If you are in Christ, the law is not for you. First Timothy 1:8,9 says that the law is for the unrighteous, for the lost. Therefore, are you willing to die to the law, and come alive to the grace of God? "For through the law I died to the law so that I might live for God" (Galatians 2:19). Your life will never be the same.

20

The Mirror of the Law

So the law was put in charge to lead us to Christ that we might be justified by faith. Now that faith has come, we are no longer under the supervision of the law.

Galatians 3:24,25

What is the purpose of the law? The answer to this question is one of the biggest misunderstandings of the Christian life. "What are we to be led by?" and "Aren't we to be led by the law as Christians?" are two questions often asked.

Scripture says, "We also know that law is made not for the righteous but for lawbreakers and rebels, the ungodly and sinful..." (1 Timothy 1:9). In its proper role, the law provides a means by which man can see his true spiritual condition. The law is like a mirror. The mirror can show you that your face is dirty, but it cannot wash your face for you. So it is with the law. It shows us that we are sinful and spiritually dead, but offers no solution to either.

Not only do we see our hopeless condition, but we also realize we are like a man without arms. We see our reflection and our need for cleansing, but we are helpless to do anything about it. If our face is going to get cleansed, then someone else will have to do the job.

That's why Galatians 3:24 says that the purpose of the law is to lead us to Christ.

Why does the law lead us to Christ? Because it is powerless to save us. The law cannot make us righteous, nor can it give life. But God in His mercy and grace designed the law to lead us to the One who can.

> Know that a man is not justified by observing the law, but by faith in Jesus Christ. So we, too, have put our faith in Christ Jesus that we may be justified by faith in Christ and not by observing the law, because by observing the law no one will be justified (Galatians 2:16).

> I found that the very commandment that was intended to bring life actually brought death (Romans 7:10).

The law demands perfection. Since we are all born in sin, it is impossible for anyone to live up to the perfection of the law. Our only hope is to turn to Christ, who alone can redeem us. If the law has done its work (led us to Christ) and as a result faith has come, then the purpose of the law has been perfectly fulfilled. Therefore, if we have been justified by grace through faith: "Now that faith has come, we are no longer under the supervision of the law" (Galatians 3:25).

When we, by faith, accept Christ's once-for-all payment for sin and receive His very life, our identity is no longer that of a filthy, wretched sinner. Our new identity is that of a child of God—a forgiven saint. We no longer have to live by law to try and make ourselves acceptable to God. Because of Christ, we have been made acceptable before God.

So what place does the law have? To show us our sinfulness in comparison to the righteous requirements of a holy God. When the law has done its work and led us to Christ, then it has fulfilled its function and purpose, and we never need to look into that mirror again. We are now led inwardly by the Holy Spirit.

Are you resting in what Christ has already done for you, or are you trying to make yourself acceptable to God by living under law? Look in the mirror and see yourself as you really are, then turn to Christ and see yourself from His perspective.

21

The City Dog and the Country Dog

*For through the law I died to the law
so that I might live for God.*

Galatians 2:19

Titus 2:12,13 says that the grace of God "teaches us to say 'No' to ungodliness and worldly passions, and to live self-controlled, upright and godly lives in this present age, while we wait for the blessed hope—the glorious appearing of our great God and Savior, Jesus Christ." For some reason we don't believe that the grace of God is teaching us to say no. We think that our obedience to the law is what produces godly living.

The law we follow is not necessarily the Ten Commandments, either. We make up our own rules and regulations for godly living. The Bible tells us, however, that "the power of sin is the law" (1 Corinthians 15:56). What we think will produce godly living actually does the opposite. It is no wonder that so many Christians live defeated lives and that many either give up or totally rebel. The difference between what the law produces and what the grace of God produces in our lives reminds me of the difference between a city dog and a country dog.

A city dog has a good life. He's got his own doghouse in the backyard. Normally, he has a full bowl of water. He is fed a couple of times a day. He can sleep all day if he

wants. He gets patted on the head and scratched behind the ears. This city dog is well taken care of.

With all the comforts at his disposal in the backyard, you would think that this city dog would want to stay at home. But what does this city dog live to do? To get outside the fence!

All you have to do is crack the gate just a little and you will see this black nose squeezing through. If you are not on your toes, the dog is out the gate before you know what's happened. Then he runs. Of course you try to catch the dumb thing, but the faster you run the faster he gets. And if he was like my dog, he looks back at you with his tongue hanging out like he is laughing at you.

You can ask yourself, "What's wrong? This dog has a great life." The problem is the fence. The dog may have a pretty good life in the backyard, but he is not free. Because he is not free, all he wants to do is get out.

That is what happens when we try to live under the law. It feels like living inside a fence. On the surface, we may look like we have a pretty good life. But on the inside, there is no freedom. The reason is that it is impossible to live up to the law, or any set of rules and regulations. And the harder we try, the more condemned and in bondage we feel. Eventually we become like the city dog, living to get out from under the law.

By contrast, go out to a farm where there are no fences. Where do you find the country dog? On the front porch...all day long. You can't get the dumb thing off. There aren't any fences. He is free and can go any place he wants, but he stays on the porch. He is lying on the porch of his master, waiting for him to come out, pet him on the head, and put him in the pickup and take him somewhere.

He is resting at the foot of his master. How come? Because there are no fences around. A country dog is totally free. He could run all over the farm if he so desired. Yet he chooses to rest on his master's porch.

That is what the grace of God does in our lives. Under the grace of God, we have total freedom to do whatever we so desire. First Corinthians 6:12 tells us, "Everything is permissible." Knowing that we are free, however, doesn't make us live like the city dog. It makes us approach life like the country dog. You see, it is the grace of God that knocks the fences down and enables us to fall in love with our Master.

That is the difference between law and grace. God never intended for us to live under the law. As a matter of fact, He says that those who are under the law are under a curse: "All who rely on observing the law are under a curse, for it is written: 'Cursed is everyone who does not continue to do everything written in the Book of the Law'" (Galatians 3:10). He gave us the law to condemn us and point us to the grace of God found in Jesus Christ. And as Galatians 3:25 states: "Now that faith has come, we are no longer under the supervision of the law."

We are no longer under the law, because the law cannot produce the Christian life. Only the grace of God can do that. In your own life you must decide whether you will live under law or under grace.

Paul said, "I do not set aside the grace of God, for if righteousness could be gained through the law, Christ died for nothing!" (Galatians 2:21). Are you setting aside the grace of God by believing that it takes the law to produce godly living?

If so, are you willing to die to the law and rest confidently in the grace of God to teach you to say "No!" and to live a righteous, upright life? It's your choice. You can continue to live as a city dog cooped up inside a fence, or you can live as a country dog, totally free and resting at the foot of the Master.

Part 7

Dependency

22

For Me to Live Is Mom

For to me to live is Christ....

Philippians 1:21

God has provided numerous illustrations on a physical level to help us understand spiritual truth. One such illustration that is especially meaningful to me was provided through the birth of my grandson, Robert.

When my two children were born, I was so wrapped up in my business that I missed much of the childbirth experience. With little Robert, however, I was very interested in learning everything I could about the development of this new life.

My son-in-law, John, is a physician. Through my conversations with John, I learned a lot about pregnancy, childbirth, and babies that I did not know before. The more we talked, the more fascinated I became with the whole childbirth process. What really caught my attention, however, was the baby's growth inside the mother.

Inside the womb, the baby is totally surrounded by water. A baby surviving in water! How could this be? Fish live in water, not humans. I jokingly asked, "Debbie is not going to have a fish, is she?" The baby does survive in this sack of water, however, because it is attached to its mother by the umbilical cord. Through the umbilical cord, the mother provides everything the baby needs. The life of the baby is sustained through the life of the mother.

If the mother stopped breathing, so would the baby. If the mother's heart stopped beating, so would the baby's. If the mother did not eat, the baby would not receive nourishment. The baby is totally dependent upon its mother. Because of this dependent relationship on the mother, the baby in the womb could say, "For me to live is Mom."

This parallels our relationship with Christ. In this world, we are totally dependent upon Jesus Christ for our very life. He revealed this profound truth to His disciples when He said, "Because I live, you also will live" (John 14:19). If He were to lose His eternal life, we would lose our eternal life. His life is what sustains us.

We experience Christ's life through the Holy Spirit. Like the umbilical cord, He is our lifeline. And through the Holy Spirit, Christ provides us everything we need to experience the abundant life He promised. Therefore, like the baby in the womb, we can say, "For to me, to live is Christ" (Philippians 1:21). This is the attitude that Christ wants each of us to adopt. The Christian life is a life of dependency. While on earth, Jesus demonstrated this life of dependency. In John 5:30, Jesus said, "By myself I can do nothing." Certainly, as God, Jesus could and can do all things, but when the "word became flesh," Jesus chose to live as a man.

As a man, Jesus lived in total dependency upon His Father. He did nothing on His own initiative. When He spoke, He said what the Father told Him to say (John 8:28). In the same way, He did only what the Father told Him to do (John 5:19). He described this life of dependency in John 14:10 when He said, "It is the Father, living in me, who is doing His work."

Just as Jesus lived in total dependency upon His Father, we are to live in total dependency upon Jesus Christ. That is why Paul wrote, "I have been crucified with Christ and I no longer live, but Christ lives in me. The life I live in the body, I live by faith in the Son of God, who loved me and gave Himself for me" (Galatians 2:20). It is Christ who lives in us and is doing His work. Our role is to live by faith and adopt an attitude of total dependency upon Christ to live His life through us.

For me, there is no better illustration of the Christian life than a baby in the womb. It can truly say, "For me to live is Mom." This is a reminder that my life is derived from Jesus Christ. If you are in Christ and Christ is in you, like the baby, you can say, "For me to live is Christ."

23

Floating

*I have been crucified with Christ and I no longer live,
but Christ lives in me. The life I live in the body, I live by faith
in the Son of God, who loved me and gave Himself for me.*

Galatians 2:20

Have you ever tried to float? If you have, you know that the harder you try to float, the faster you sink. Have you tried to live the Christian life? It is just like trying to float. It seems impossible! The harder you try to live the Christian life, the worse you do. The key to both, however, is in not trying at all.

My dad taught me the key to floating as a kid. On our summer vacations to the beach, he spent most of his time floating in the ocean. He stretched out, put his arms behind his head, and floated for hours at a time. Every time I tried, however, I sank right to the bottom. I asked, "Dad, how do you do that?" His answer was, "I'm not actually doing anything at all. I'm just relaxing out there." After numerous attempts to float, I finally learned the key. My job was merely to surrender my body to the water. *It was the water's job to hold me up.*

So it is with the Christian life. We cannot live the Christian life; only Christ can. Paul explained this in Galatians 2:20: "I have been crucified with Christ and I no longer live, but Christ lives in me. The life I live in the body, I live by faith in the Son of God, who loved me and gave Himself for me."

Just as it is the water's job to hold us up in floating, it is Christ's job to live the Christian life through us. Our role is merely to surrender to Him and let Him live His life. This is the key to the Christian life.

This truth is so simple that most people ask, "What are we supposed to do if Christ does all the work?" The above verse says that we are to live by faith. We are to trust Jesus to do exactly what He has promised to do: to live His life. That is all we can do. Jesus made that very clear when He said, "Apart from me you can do nothing" (John 15:5). We have no other option in the Christian life except to trust Jesus Christ.

The Christian life is characterized by love, joy, peace, patience, kindness, goodness, faithfulness, gentleness, and self-control (Galatians 5:22,23). This is the fruit of the Spirit that Christ produces in our lives. It is impossible for us to produce the fruit of the Spirit through our own strength. As hard as we may try, love, joy, or peace will not be the end result of our efforts. Trying to produce these qualities is like trying to float. It doesn't work.

For example, have you ever tried to love an enemy or to experience the peace of God that passes understanding in the midst of rejection or a bad circumstance? How successful were you? It is not hard to live the Christian life. It is impossible! That is why our only option is to trust the One who can. And believe it or not, this is what pleases God. "And without faith it is impossible to please God" (Hebrews 11:6).

God never called us to "gut out" the Christian life. We cannot live it even when we try. Recognize this fact and then make the intelligent decision to trust Jesus Christ. He is alive and has promised to live His life in and through you.

People at the beach would see my dad out in the water and say, "Look at that guy floating." My dad took all the credit for floating, but he knew that he wasn't holding himself afloat. It was the water doing all the work. In the same way, people might think you are producing the Christian life. But if anything good is coming out of you, it is Christ who is doing the work.

Are you tired of trying to live the Christian life? If so, are you willing to recognize that apart from Christ you can do nothing, and then trust Jesus Christ, the One who has promised to live the Christian life through you? In so doing you will begin to experience the abundant life that Jesus promised.

24

The Pack and the Pickup

Come to Me, all you who are weary and burdened, and I will give you rest. Take My yoke upon you and learn from Me, for I am gentle and humble in heart, and you will find rest for your souls. For My yoke is easy and My burden is light.

Matthew 11:28-30

Do you ever hear Christians talk about how hard it is to live the Christian life? The Christian life is not *difficult* to live; it is *impossible*. Most Christians try, however, to live the Christian life through their own strength. They live as practical atheists.

A practical atheist is someone who, when he encounters a problem in life, meets it as if he is the only resource available. This person reminds me of the story of the pickup truck and the hitchhiker.

A man is driving his pickup truck down the road when he sees a hitchhiker carrying a heavy load. He pulls over and offers a ride, which the hitchhiker gladly accepts.

A little way down the road, the driver looks in his rearview mirror and notices that the hitchhiker is hunched over in the bed of the truck and still carrying his heavy load over his shoulder. The driver stops and says, "Hey, buddy, why don't you put the sack down on the bed of the truck?"

"That's okay," responds the hitchhiker. "I don't want to bother you that much. Just take me to my destination and I will be happy."

How ridiculous! But this is the attitude of many Christians. They happily board the Lord's "salvation wagon" that will take them to heaven, but they shoulder the effort along the way.

What a contrast this attitude is to the words of Jesus:

> Come to Me, all you who are weary and burdened, and I will give you rest. Take My yoke upon you and learn from Me, for I am gentle and humble in heart, and you will find rest for your souls. For My yoke is easy and My burden is light (Matthew 11:28-30).

Jesus does not expect us to carry our own burdens in this life. As a matter of fact, Peter tells us to "Cast all your anxiety on Him because He cares for you" (1 Peter 5:7). The Christian life is getting in the yoke with Jesus and allowing Him to carry our cares.

In other words, the Christian life is all up to Christ. Not only is He responsible for getting us to heaven, but He is also responsible for carrying us through this life on earth. And He is certainly big enough to handle any circumstance that we may face.

Therefore, we should live in total dependency upon Him in every area of life. We are to live in total dependence on Christ, trusting that He will cause "all things to work together for good" (Romans 8:28 NASB) and that His "grace is sufficient" (2 Corinthians 12:9) for any trial encountered in life.

You don't have to live as a practical atheist. The Christian life begins in faith and is lived by faith in Jesus Christ. Make it your aim to experience the abundant life that Jesus has promised through a life of total dependence upon Him and His love and grace.

Truth

25

Follow Facts Instead of Fantasy

Do not be anxious about anything, but in everything, by prayer and petition, with thanksgiving, present your requests to God. And the peace of God, which transcends all understanding, will guard your hearts and your minds in Christ Jesus.

Philippians 4:6,7

We have all heard the saying "If it feels good, do it!" This modern-day philosophy makes our feelings or emotions the criteria for truth. Truth, however, is not and cannot be determined by feelings. God has so engineered man that our emotions are merely responders to what we are thinking. The book of Proverbs puts it this way: "As [a man] thinks within himself, so he is" (Proverbs 23:7 NASB).

It has always been that way, and as long as we function in a body of flesh on this earth, it always will be. Whatever I'm thinking will determine the way I feel. Emotions always follow thought. That is the way we have been designed by God.

Emotions have no ability to think on their own. They cannot reason. They cannot discern the past from the future or the future from the present. Neither can they discern truth from error. They always predictably respond to what we allow into our minds through our eye gates, our ear gates, or through our thinking patterns, whether proper or improper.

Most of us have been to a scary movie at one time or another. There were probably dozens of other people in the theater with you, and before you sat down you knew that you would be seeing a staged event. It would not be real—only images created by light projected through a long strip of film. Yet when *Jaws* jumped out of that water, your heart practically leaped out of your chest. Whether you are a man or woman, it mattered little at that point as you shrieked at the top of your lungs (or wanted to)!

Emotions are like that. They are dumb. They can't discern the real from the imaginary. They didn't know that what you were seeing was fiction. They just predictably responded to what came into your mind through your eyes and your ears.

When I was younger, I went with my brother and sister to see what was (up to that time) one of the most horrifying motion pictures ever produced. Intellectually, I knew it wasn't real, but when Psycho tore into that shower, I crawled under my seat in sheer terror! I practically embarrassed my brother and sister to death. Why did I react that way? My emotions did not know that I wasn't in that shower with Psycho. They could not tell fact from fiction, and they began to run wild.

Our emotional state will always be related directly to what we are thinking. We cannot subject our eyes and ears to scenes of horror and experience peaceful serenity at the same time. We cannot dwell on angry thoughts and at the same time experience joy in our hearts. We cannot dwell on sad thoughts without being overtaken by sadness. Nor can we dwell on depressing thoughts and not expect ultimately to become depressed.

God gave us a mind, and what we allow to come into it will dictate our emotional responses. Whether what we see and hear is fact or fantasy, whether what we are considering is truth or error, whether we are contemplating the past, future, or present, our emotions will respond to what we are thinking. They have no choice.

Typically, the way we operate is that we think something, feel something, and then do something. Our actions are a direct result of what we are feeling. If we are to experience freedom in our lives, however, we must let truth, not our feelings, determine our actions. From God's vantage point, we should think something, act on it by faith, and then we can experience the emotions God wants us to experience.

Philippians 4:6,7 is an example of this:

> Do not be anxious about anything, but in everything, by prayer and petition, with thanksgiving, present your requests to God. And the peace of God, which transcends all understanding, will guard your hearts and your minds in Christ Jesus.

It says that we are not to be anxious about anything. Now, what is anxiety? It is an emotion. You say, "Okay, Lord, what do You want me to do?" He tells you to present your requests to Him with an attitude of thanksgiving. He is the only One who can take care of the circumstances that you are anxious about. Therefore, this verse says to trust Him. And what happens? When you act upon this truth by faith, you will experience the peace of God that passes understanding. The truth of God came into your mind, you acted upon it by faith, and then you experienced peace.

The battleground for your emotions begins in the mind. If your emotions are out of control, it is not because you have emotional problems. You have thinking problems. The solution is to begin renewing your mind with truth and then acting on this truth by faith, regardless of what your emotions may be telling you to do. Romans 12:2 gives us the pattern: "Do not conform any longer to the pattern of this world, but be transformed by the renewing of your mind. Then you will be able to test and approve what God's will is—His good, pleasing and perfect will."

If you are in bondage to your emotions, recognize that your emotions are predictably responding to what you are thinking. Let God renew your mind with truth. Then you will be able to experience the peace of God that passes understanding and enjoy the freedom that is yours in Christ.

26

The Teddy Bear and the Puppy

So I say, live by the Spirit, and you will not gratify the desires of the flesh. For the flesh desires what is contrary to the Spirit, and the Spirit what is contrary to the flesh. They are in conflict with each other, so that you do not do what you want.

Galatians 5:16,17

Have you ever found yourself saying, "Why do I keep doing that?" All of us, at some time or another, have struggled with bad habits. The frustrating thing about it is, the more we try to overcome these bad habits, the more we find ourselves doing them.

What we fail to understand is that when we become preoccupied with self and focus on our shortcomings, the inevitable result is failure. When we are busy trying to clean up the flesh, where is the focus of our minds? On cleaning up the flesh. The one who sows the seed of the flesh, reaps the harvest of the flesh (Galatians 6:8). To free ourselves from bad habits,we must take our focus off of ourselves.

In Romans 7:18, Paul states flatly, "I know that nothing good lives in me, that is, in my flesh." And in the fifty-third chapter of Isaiah the prophet stated, "We all, like sheep, have gone astray, each of us has turned to his own way."

The truth of the matter is that as long as man lives in a body of flesh, sin will indwell him. How then can we purify ourselves of the very thing that indwells us? In and of ourselves, it is impossible. Therefore, the most sensible thing we can do is heed the instruction of Paul in Romans 6:11: "Count yourselves dead to sin but alive to God in Christ Jesus." The question then becomes "How do I accomplish this?"

In Galatians 5:16 (NASB), Paul provides the answer: "Walk by the Spirit, and you will not carry out the desire of the flesh." Notice that he did not say that the desires of the flesh would go away. Nor did he say to clean up the flesh so that you can walk in the Spirit. Not fulfilling the desires of the flesh is a result of walking in the Spirit.

It's like a baby in a playpen, focusing his attention on his favorite stuffed animal: a teddy bear. He holds on to that bear for dear life, and if anyone tries to take it away, that baby screams at the top of his lungs! He is focused on that bear, his security blanket, and no one is going to take it away. It is soft and cuddly. It looks back at him. And it is always there, waiting for a hug.

How in the world can we ever shift this child's dependency off the teddy bear? Easy. Get him a puppy. Just drop a puppy in the playpen and watch what happens. This puppy is warm. It wiggles, moves around, makes sounds, and wags its tail 90 miles an hour. When he pets it, the puppy licks him back—even seems to like him. Why, this is great! Who needs that dumb bear anymore? This puppy is alive! It's a lot more fun than a stuffed animal.

Once the child has become preoccupied with the puppy, all you need to do is reach into the playpen and take the teddy bear out. The baby won't even realize it is gone.

So it is with bad habits. Fall in love with Jesus, get preoccupied with His life, then you will see the bad habits simply going away. If you want to let go of a bad habit, then get your eyes on Jesus. It is not enough to tell people what they should stop doing. They must develop a totally new mind-set—a new preoccupation. We are not able to let go of things until we have something new to hang on to.

Are there bad habits in your life that you have been trying to get rid of? If so, forget about the habit and focus your attention on Christ. Soon you will experience what Paul discussed in Galatians 5:16 (NASB): "Walk by the Spirit, and you will not carry out the desire of the flesh."

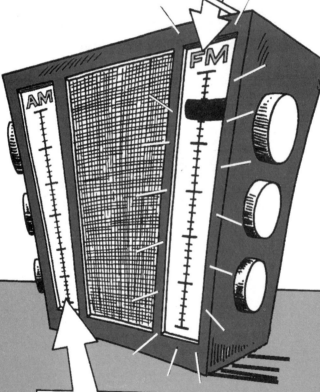

27

The AM-FM Radio

Do not conform any longer to the pattern of this world,
but be transformed by the renewing of your mind.
Then you will be able to test and approve what
God's will is—His good, pleasing and perfect will.

Romans 12:2

Within every Christian are both the desires of the flesh and the desires of the Spirit. Paul tells us in Galatians 5:17 that these desires are in conflict one with another. We all know this to be true. If someone insults us, our flesh wants to get back at that person, but the Spirit of God living inside says to forgive. Which desire do we follow? This is a battle that every Christian encounters, and this battle begins in the mind.

Our mind functions in such a way that it can be compared to an AM-FM radio. An AM-FM radio has been designed to receive both AM and FM signals. The AM signal carries programming that can only be heard on the AM dial; and the FM signal carries programming that can only be heard on the FM dial. A radio listener does not have a choice as to the programming on either signal. He does have a choice, however, as to which signal (AM or FM) he will listen to. So it is with our minds.

We have been created in such a way that our minds can receive input from both Satan and the world, and from God and His Word. The programming on the AM dial of our mind comes from Satan and the world. Satan and the world fill our minds with lies or error that appeal to the flesh and its desires. "For everything in the world—the cravings of sinful man, the lust of his eyes and the boasting of what he has and does—comes not from the Father but from the world" (1 John 2:16).

The programming on the FM dial of our minds comes from God and His Word. This is *truth* that appeals to the Spirit and its desires. However, as it is written:

> "No eye has seen, no ear has heard, no mind has conceived what God has prepared for those who love Him"—but God has revealed it to us by His Spirit....We have not received the spirit of the world but the Spirit who is from God, that we may understand what God has freely given us (1 Corinthians 2:9,10,12).

Just like the radio, we cannot change the programming that comes from Satan, nor can we change the programming that comes from God. However, we can choose whether we will listen to Satan and his error or God and His truth.

Jesus said in John 8:31,32, "If you hold to my teaching, you are really my disciples. Then you will know the truth, and the truth will set you free." If truth sets you free, then error must put you in bondage. If you choose to listen to Satan and the world, you will experience bondage. If you choose to listen to God and His Word, you will experience freedom.

The error that comes from Satan says:

- to worry about everything
- you have to be a lot better than that
- to analyze why you are so bad
- you deserve to be treated better than that
- you will not be happy until you get _____
- to blame people for your problems

- to wonder what tomorrow will bring

Truth, on the other hand, that comes from God says:

- "Be anxious for nothing" (Philippians 4:6 NASB).
- "By one sacrifice, He has made you perfect forever" (Hebrews 10:14).
- "Consider yourselves to be dead to sin, but alive to God" (Romans 6:11 NASB).
- Love "does not take into account a wrong suffered" (1 Corinthians 13:5 NASB).
- "I have learned to be content whatever the circumstances" (Philippians 4:11).
- "Take the log out of your own eye" (Matthew 7:5 NASB).
- "Do not be anxious for tomorrow; for tomorrow will care for itself" (Matthew 6:34 NASB).

For a Christian, whom to listen to seems like an easy choice. Who in their right mind would choose bondage over freedom? We do, however. Why? Because our emotions respond to whatever is in our minds. Satan gets his programming into our minds through our five senses. And what we see, hear, feel, taste, or smell produces an emotional response. It is in this emotional response that the desires of the flesh are cultivated. At this point, because we are so feelings-oriented, it becomes very easy to act out the desires of the flesh.

Truth, however, is not determined by feelings. Just because we feel something doesn't mean it is true. We are, therefore, not to let feelings dictate what our actions will be. That is why the Bible tells us not to conform any longer "to the pattern of this world, but be transformed by the renewing of your mind. Then you will be able to test and approve what God's will is—His good, pleasing and perfect will" (Romans 12:2).

Jesus Christ lives inside each believer and is constantly feeding truth into our minds in every circumstance we encounter. Jesus Christ is there to remind us of our identity in Christ, of His constant love and forgiveness, and of the sufficiency of His grace. Based on the truth of His love and grace, He reasons with us and then asks us to present our bodies to Him regardless of what our emotions are telling us to do.

> Therefore, I urge you, brothers, in view of God's mercy, to offer your bodies as living sacrifices, holy and pleasing to God—this is your spiritual act of worship (Romans 12:1).

> Do not offer the parts of your body to sin, as instruments of wickedness, but rather offer yourselves to God, as those who have been brought from death to life; and offer the parts of your body to Him as instruments of righteousness (Romans 6:13).

When we do, we will be able to test and approve God's will—His good, pleasing, and perfect will.

Whether you experience bondage or God's will (freedom) is determined by whether you listen to Satan and his error or to God and His truth. To which dial will you tune your mind?

Part
9

Freedom

28

The Cafeteria

For sin shall not be your master, because you are not under law, but under grace. What then? Shall we sin because we are not under law but under grace? By no means!

Romans 6:14,15

Whenever the pure message of God's love and acceptance in Jesus Christ is taught, one objection is always raised: "You are giving people a license to sin." This objection is not new. In fact, Paul asked and answered this objection in his letter to the Romans. "What shall we say, then? Shall we go on sinning so that grace may increase?...What then? Shall we sin because we are not under law but under grace?" (Romans 6:1,15).

To both questions Paul's answer is "By no means!" It's as if he were saying, "What an absurd question!" And it is an absurd question when you understand the love and grace of God and know that Christ lives in you.

Imagine that you own a fine cafeteria. One day you hear a tremendous commotion in the alley where the garbage dumpsters are. There you find the most pitiful-looking human being you have ever seen fighting with several stray cats over the food scraps in the dumpster.

Moved with compassion, you approach the guy and say, "Listen, I can't stand to see you eating garbage. Come into my cafeteria and eat."

"I don't have any money," he replies.

"It doesn't matter. You can eat at my cafeteria every day absolutely free of charge." Taking the guy by the arm, you lead him inside. There in front of him are vegetables...salads...fruits...beef...fish...chicken...cakes...pies. "Eat anything you want," you say. "It's yours for the taking."

With unbelieving eyes he asks, "Do you really mean that I can eat anything I want?"

"Yes, you may eat anything you want."

Standing in front of the most fabulous spread of food he could imagine, with the offer to eat anything for free, what if the guy looked at you and asked, "Can I go back to the dumpster and eat more garbage?" You would think the guy was crazy. In the face of all that delicious food, all he can think to ask is whether he can eat garbage. How ridiculous!

Jesus Christ laid down His life for us to take away our sins and to free us from the bondage of sin and death. Then, raised from the dead, Jesus gave us His very life to experience: a life characterized by love, joy, peace, patience, kindness, goodness, faithfulness, gentleness, and self-control. And in the face of a "cafeteria line" like this, that Jesus called "abundant" life (John 10:10 NASB), all some of us can think to ask is, "Does that mean that I can go out and sin more?" In other words, "Can I continue eating garbage?"

Somehow we have missed the goal of the Christian life. We are obsessed with sin. Most of our preaching and teaching is directed toward getting people to quit sinning. In our analogy, instead of saying to the starving man, "Come and eat," most Christian teaching would say, "Stay out of the garbage! Don't eat the garbage!" It is no wonder that we are more interested in garbage than we are in cafeteria food.

First Corinthians 15:56 says, "The sting of death is sin, and the power of sin is the law." Like the garbage, sin looks pretty good when you constantly hear, "Don't sin. You have to quit sinning." That is why the goal of the Christian life is not to quit sinning. Jesus did not come so that we would quit sinning. He came that we might "have life, and have it to the full" (John 10:10).

Garbage will lose its appeal to our starving man once he gets into the cafeteria line and begins experiencing what good food tastes like. In the same way, sin loses its appeal once a person begins to experience the very life of Christ. The life of Christ is what every human being needs. We need to experience daily the reality of knowing Christ and walking with Him in a vibrant relationship. The Lord defined eternal life this way: "Now this is eternal life: that they may know You, the only true God, and Jesus Christ, whom You have sent" (John 17:3). That is the real goal of the Christian life: knowing Christ!

It is only in comparison with the riches of knowing Christ that sin begins to lose its appeal. As a matter of fact, sin becomes stupid. It is so dumb to settle for anything less than experiencing Jesus Christ Himself. Why should you ever wallow in the garbage when the Lord has provided a banquet table?

No, the grace of God does not give us a license to sin. The grace of God frees us from the bondage of sin and death and allows us to experience the very life of Christ. We are beloved, accepted children of God, who have been called to His banquet table to experience Jesus Christ living in and through us every day. Abundant life is not "pie in the sky." It is real, and it is ours for the taking if we will only believe. Let's not settle for anything less.

29

Monkeying Around

To the Jews who had believed Him, Jesus said, "If you hold to My teaching, you are really My disciples. Then you will know the truth, and the truth will set you free."

John 8:31,32

Much of the Christian world lives in spiritual bondage today. The reason is that we hold to misconceptions concerning what the Christian life is all about. Our misconceptions range from our understanding of forgiveness and identity in Christ to how we are supposed to live the Christian life every day. Regardless of what the misconceptions are, they do not line up with the truth of God and His Word.

The way that we hold to these misconceptions and remain in spiritual bondage reminds me of how monkeys are captured in the tropics. The natives hollow out a coconut, fill the coconut with sweet beans, and then attach it to the base of a tree. After dark, the monkey comes by and notices the sweet beans in the coconut. He reaches in through the hole in the coconut and takes hold of the beans. In grabbing the beans, the monkey makes a fist that is too large to remove. He won't let go of the beans, and he can't take his hand out of the coconut. So the monkey just sits there. The next morning the natives come by and pick the dumb thing up still holding onto his beans.

All the monkey had to do to go free was let go of the sweet beans. And so it is with us. All we have to do to go free in our Christian experience is let go of the misconceptions we are grasping concerning the Christian life. This is the point Jesus was making to the Pharisees when He said, "If you hold to My teaching, you are really My disciples. Then you will know the truth, and the truth will set you free" (John 8:31-32).

Several years ago, when I was involved in the busiest Christian schedule you could imagine and experiencing burnout, that verse came to mind. I was busy doing things for the Lord, but I was barren and didn't know why. My Christian life felt more like a job than a relationship with the living God. It suddenly occurred to me that if truth sets you free, the opposite had to be true: Error puts you in bondage. I knew that I wasn't free, and there was only one reason why: I was living according to error rather than according to truth.

Once I identified this—truth sets you free; error binds you—my next thought was to ask, "What error have I grabbed hold of concerning the Christian life?" As I have said, my life was busy and barren. I used to tell people that "Christianity is not a religion; it's a relationship with God through His Son, Jesus Christ." The joy of my salvation left because I had strayed from my relationship with God back to practicing a religion. That was the error I was grasping.

What was the solution? Just like the monkey, all I had to do was to let go of the error and start believing truth. I asked the Lord to teach me the truth that He promised would set me free. And that is what He did. He showed me afresh that Christianity is not a religion. It is a relationship. John describes it this way: "Now this is eternal life: that they may know You, the only true God, and Jesus Christ, whom You have sent" (John 17:3). Today my relationship with God is even more exciting than when it first began.

What about your relationship with Christ? Are you in bondage today? If so, it is because you are holding on to error concerning the Christian life. Are you willing to let go and let God teach you the truth that will set you free? Nothing good can come from holding onto something that is keeping you from experiencing the abundance of life that God has promised, and experiencing day by day the freedom that is found only in Christ Jesus our Lord.

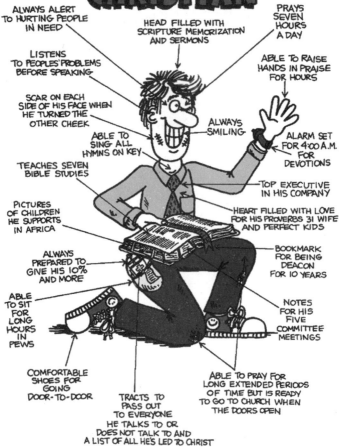

30

The Phantom Christian

*Accept one another, then, just as Christ accepted you,
in order to bring praise to God.*

Romans 15:7

Most Christians can quote John 3:16: "For God so loved the world..." Yet, many Christians walk around every day feeling that God is sick to His stomach because of their failure to live up to His standards. Often, though, it's not even God's standards that Christians are trying to keep, but regulations imposed by themselves or other people. They are trying to be like what I like to call the "Phantom Christian."

The Phantom Christian is that imaginary person to whom many of us are continually comparing ourselves. He is the superspiritual man who gets up every day at 4:00 A.M. to pray for several hours. Then he reads his Bible for several hours. He goes to work (at which he is tops in his field), where he effectively shares Christ with everyone in his office. He teaches several Bible studies, goes to church every time the doors are open, and serves on several committees. He is also a wonderful spiritual leader at home—a sterling example of a loving husband and father, who leads stimulating family devotions every day for his "Proverbs 31 wife" and perfect children.

Of course no one could live up to such a standard. Even if some person had the ability, he would still need 100 hours in a day! Rationally, we all know that the

Phantom Christian is ridiculous, but somehow he remains in the back of our minds, creating in us a sense of failure to measure up. That is the reason why many, many Christians live under continual guilt. For those who believe that the Phantom Christian is God's standard for acceptance, God seems a million miles away, sitting in heaven with His arms folded in disapproval.

People in this bondage know well the biblical teaching that God loves them, but they clearly do not believe in their hearts that God accepts them. And apart from knowing about and resting in God's acceptance, His love becomes practically meaningless and irrelevant in daily living. I have often talked of God's love in counseling appointments and seen Christians react bitterly to the words. "So what?" they say. "He loves everybody!" Apart from acceptance, God's love becomes some kind of vague, universal, impersonal love.

God's standard of acceptance is certainly not the Phantom Christian. His standards are much higher than that. For us to be acceptable in God's sight, only the righteousness of Christ will do. And that is what every child of God has been given in Christ. "God made Him who had no sin to be sin for us, so that in Him we might become the righteousness of God" (2 Corinthians 5:21). If you are a true Christian, then you are as righteous and acceptable as Jesus Christ.

When I teach about our acceptance in Christ, I usually ask a series of questions to help drive home the truth that God accepts us just for who we are right now. "How many of you," I ask, "are as righteous and acceptable as I am in the sight of God?" Believe it or not, most hands go up. "How many of you are as righteous and acceptable in the sight of God as Billy Graham?" Usually about half the audience raise their hands to answer this question. Next I ask, "How many of you are as righteous and acceptable in the sight of God as the apostle Paul?" Only about ten percent of the people respond to this question. Now here's the really tough one: "How many of you are as righteous and acceptable in the sight of God as Jesus Christ?" Very few hands normally go up. Why? Because we still think that our acceptance is based upon our performance—on how well we are living up to the standard of the Phantom Christian.

How could I stand up and say that I am as righteous and acceptable in the sight of God as Jesus Christ? Because of what I do? No way! It is because of what He has done. He made me righteous and acceptable in His sight. As long as you think that your acceptance is based on your performance, you will never grow in your Christian life. The truth, however, is that God sees you as totally acceptable in His sight right now—not because of what you do, but because of what Christ has done for you. Romans 15:7 puts it this way: "Accept one another, then, just as Christ accepted you, in order to bring praise to God." If you are in Christ, then through God's grace you are totally acceptable in God's sight.

You no longer have to try to be the Phantom Christian. You are already as righteous as Jesus Christ. Because of this, it is my prayer that you will never again wrestle with God's acceptance of you, so that you can go on to discover the immeasurable wonders of His love.

31

Under Construction

Being confident of this, that He who began a good work in you will carry it on to completion until the day of Christ Jesus.

Philippians 1:6

It is so easy to judge people and say, "I can't believe he/she did that. I would never do something like that." The Bible warns against this type of attitude. Paul wrote to the Galatians saying, "Brothers, if someone is caught in a sin, you who are spiritual should restore him gently. But watch yourself, or you also may be tempted" (Galatians 6:1).

All of us are capable of committing any sin mentioned in the Bible, given the right circumstances. That is why Paul warns against an attitude of condemnation toward other people. "Watch yourself, or you also may be tempted." Because each of us struggles with the desires of the flesh, we need to adopt an attitude of restoration toward other people, realizing that God continues to work in each of our lives. It is like God has put a big sign on the front of each of us which reads Under Construction.

When you and I come to Christ by faith, we are born again of the Spirit of God and we become new creatures in Christ. What is new, however, is the spiritual part of man. Neither our bodies nor our souls are born again.

We still look the same on the outside, and we are capable of thinking, feeling, and doing the same dumb stuff we did when we were lost. The difference is that now Christ has come to live inside each of us through the person of the Holy Spirit, and He has left us with the promise "that He who began a good work in you will carry it on to completion until the day of Christ Jesus" (Philippians 1:6).

God is not finished with any of us yet. He will complete the work He began in us, and His work is to conform us to the image of His Son. The apostle John writes, "Dear friends, now we are children of God, and what we will be has not yet been made known. But we know that when He appears, we shall be like Him, for we shall see Him as He is" (1 John 3:2). When we see Jesus, we will be like Him. This is the hope that we have here and now—not only for ourselves, but for one another.

Even when we struggle with the desires of the flesh, God is at work in our lives. Our struggles do not surprise Him. He lives in us and, whether we struggle or not, He continues to conform us to His image. That is what He asks us to trust Him to do—not only in our lives, but in the lives of others.

We are all in the same boat. If we are to be conformed to the image of Christ, Christ will have to do it. Knowing this is what enables us to do as Paul said—to have an attitude of restoration, not condemnation, toward one another, and to see the big sign on each other's chest which reads Under Construction!

Other Books by
Bob George

Classic Christianity
Classic Christianity Study Guide
Complete in Christ
Growing in Grace with Study Guide
Victory Over Depression
Grace Stories
Faith That Pleases God

People to People
MINISTRIES

Bob George can be heard live each weekday on *People to People!*

The longest-running live national call-in
biblical counseling program on Christian radio.

Bob George, host
of *People to People*

Live!
Monday – Friday
3:30 P.M. – 4:00 P.M. *CST*
6:05 P.M. – 7:00 P.M. *CST*

For a listing of radio stations in your area,
call **1-800-727-2828,** or visit us on the Internet at:
www.realanswers.net

Real Answers
for
Real Life™
Call 1-800-677-9377
to participate in the radio program.